THE 10 DUMBEST THINGS CHRISTIANS DO

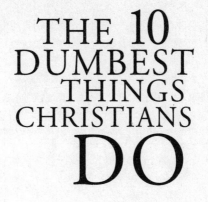

OTHER BOOKS BY MARK ATTEBERRY

Walking with God on the Road You Never Wanted to Travel

The Caleb Quest

The Samson Syndrome

THE 10 DUMBEST THINGS CHRISTIANS DO

Mark Atteberry

NELSON BOOKS
A Division of Thomas Nelson Publishers
Since 1798

www.thomasnelson.com

Published in Nashville, Tennessee, by Thomas Nelson, Inc.

Library of Congress Cataloging-in-Publication Data

Atteberry, Mark.
    The 10 dumbest things Christians do / Mark Atteberry.
       p. cm.
    Includes bibliographical references.
    ISBN 0-7852-1148-9 (pbk.)
    1. Christian life. I. Title: Ten dumbest things Christians do. II. Title.
BV4501.3.A15 2006
248.4--dc22
2005036827

Printed in the United States of America

06 07 08 09 10 RRD 6 5 4 3 2 1

For Jim Chesser, Nils Taranger,
Paul Wasmund, and Jasen Whiting

Not many people would want to have a book about dumb things dedicated to them. Let the record show that I have chosen these men, not because they do dumb things, but because they don't. They are the current elders of Poinciana Christian Church, where I have served as preaching minister for the better part of two decades. They are excellent leaders and even better friends.

CONTENTS

ix   *Acknowledgments*

xi   INTRODUCTION: The Church in Clown Shoes

1   DUMB MOVE #1: Slinging Mud on the Bride of Christ

21   DUMB MOVE #2: Winning People to the Church Rather Than to the LORD

41   DUMB MOVE #3: Living Below the Level of Our Beliefs

61   DUMB MOVE #4: Speaking Above the Level of Our Knowledge

81   DUMB MOVE #5: Hopping from Church to Church

103   DUMB MOVE #6: Fighting Among Ourselves

125   DUMB MOVE #7: Missing Golden Opportunities

143   DUMB MOVE #8: Settling for Mediocrity

163   DUMB MOVE #9: Allowing Wolves to Live Among the Sheep

183   DUMB MOVE #10: Accepting the Unacceptable

201   *A Letter from Mark*

203   *Questions for Group Discussion or Personal Reflection*

209   *Notes*

210   *About the Author*

ACKNOWLEDGMENTS

It is an honor to once again have the Nelson Books logo stamped on my work. This great company employs some of the finest, most professional people I have ever met. In particular, Brian Hampton, Kyle Olund, Bryan Norman, and Melanie Bryant have become cherished friends.

Lee Hough, of Alive Communications, is my agent, sounding board, prayer partner, and friend. There's no one I trust or respect more.

My wife, Marilyn, continues to make our home a paradise. With thirty-one years of marriage behind us, it just keeps getting better.

These incredible people walk with me—sometimes suffer with me—through every project. I am not the best writer in the world, and certainly not the biggest selling author. But I doubt that anyone who's ever put pen to paper is more blessed than I.

The Church in Clown Shoes

Right now, there's every reason to believe that several people in your church are working daily to frustrate God and hinder the progress of His kingdom. What's more, it's a pretty safe bet you're one of them.

But wait!

Before you sling this book across the room, let me explain.

I'm not suggesting that you or your friends are doing this intentionally. In fact, I suspect you're not even aware of it. In all likelihood, your love for the Lord is real, and you're living out your Christian life the best way you know how. The very idea that you're frustrating God probably horrifies you. But there's a good chance you're doing it anyway, just like me and millions of other Christians.

How?

With some really dumb moves.

But not the ones we make because of our humanity. I'm not

about to criticize anybody for occasionally reaffirming his membership in the human race by doing something less than brilliant. Ask anybody who's ever worked with me, and they'll tell you that I've messed up enough times to qualify for membership in the Knucklehead Hall of Fame. I suspect you have, too.

No, the blunders I'm referring to are the ones we tend to make again and again simply because we don't recognize them as blunders. Why don't we? I can think of three reasons. First, in some cases there's no "book, chapter, and verse" that condemns them. As a result, they're very rarely discussed, let alone denounced, from the pulpit or in print. Second, they often involve some sort of religious activity or behavior that makes it easy for us to blindly accept them. And third, they tend to be things we've done for years without anyone ever shrieking in horror, calling the cops, or telling us we can no longer serve on the deacon board. On the contrary, some of the dumb things we do actually earn us respect and hearty congratulations from other believers who are just as blind to them as we are. But dumb moves are still dumb moves whether we recognize them or not, and we desperately need to stop making them.

The reason why is illustrated by my friend Cassie.

She's a clown. Not just a witty person who livens up a party, but a real, honest-to-goodness clown. She's been to clown school, has a custom-made clown suit, a pink fuzzy wig, face paint, and hilarious clown shoes. Imagine her little size-five feet laced up inside shoes that are eighteen inches long. Those babies flip and flop when she walks, adding the perfect finishing touch to her outfit.

But when our coed softball team takes the field on Sunday afternoons and Cassie trots out to third base, she's never wearing her clown shoes. Instead, she's strapped into a spiffy pair of Nike cleats. That's not to say she *couldn't* play in her clown shoes. But if she did, she obviously wouldn't be very effective. They would slow her down at the very least, and probably have her tripping over herself and falling flat on her face in crucial situations.

As I see it, the blunders I'm going to be addressing in this book are the church's clown shoes. They're the reasons why our efforts to serve God are often woefully ineffective. They explain, at least in part, why the world has a hard time taking us seriously. And worst of all, they provide Satan with sidesplitting entertainment. Yes, I know he's whipped. I know his fate was sealed when Jesus came out of the tomb. But I still have to believe he roars with laughter, high-fives his demons, and thumbs his nose at God when he sees some of the dumb things we do again and again.

I'm sure he's hoping we never figure out what we're doing wrong. He's hoping it never dawns on us why our valiant efforts to serve God often bear so little fruit. He's hoping we never realize that we could be bouncing around in a sleek pair of Nikes instead of bumbling and stumbling in our clown shoes. He knows that if we ever wake up, the laughs will stop and his work will instantly become a lot more difficult. He'll have to start digging for ammunition to use against us instead of having us serve it to him on a silver platter.

If you agree that it's time for the church to take off its clown shoes and slip into a pair of Nikes . . . and if you'd like to help that transition along in your own little corner of the kingdom . . . keep reading. I'm going to identify what I believe are the ten dumbest things we do to frustrate God and keep the devil in stitches. I'll explain why these blunders are so devastating, try my best to correct the ideas and attitudes that perpetuate them, and, hopefully, set us off on a course that'll have us acting a little more like the three wise men and a little less like the Three Stooges.

I doubt that you'll have made all of these blunders, but it wouldn't surprise me if several of the chapters you're about to read will cause the color to rise in your cheeks. I have no problem admitting that I've made quite a few of these mistakes myself. Just remember that there's often no ill intent behind these blunders. So the goal here is not to condemn or shame anyone. We simply need to understand what we're doing wrong and make the necessary corrections. The calling God has placed on us to seek and save the lost is challenging enough as it is. We certainly don't want to make it more difficult by doing things that knock the shine off our witness and turn hungry hearts away.

The apostle Paul said, "We try to live in such a way that no one will be hindered from finding the Lord by the way we act, and so no one can find fault with our ministry" (2 Corinthians 6:3 NLT). If there's a theme verse for this book, that's it. Recently, I took it a step further and made it the theme verse of my life. I decided it was high time I got rid of my clown shoes. I've made up my mind that if God is going to roll His eyes and shake His head in exasperation, it will no longer be because of me. And if Satan is going to fall down laughing, it won't be because of my bumbling and stumbling. If you, too, are ready to change your shoes, keep reading.

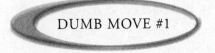

Slinging Mud on the Bride of Christ

To be a critic, you have to have maybe three percent education, five percent intelligence, two percent style, and ninety percent gall.

—JUDITH CRIST

During my thirty-two years in the ministry, I've officiated at well over one hundred weddings. While I don't remember most of them, I must tell you there are a few I'll never forget. Like the one where the bride fell down . . . in the mud.

It was about an hour before the ceremony. The wedding party had gone outside with the photographer to find a pretty spot for some pictures. They found one, but it meant walking through a small depression made squishy by some early morning showers. Everyone stepped lightly and hiked up their pant legs and dresses, making it into position without incident.

It was the return trip that brought disaster.

1

The bride, walking on her tiptoes in shoes she wasn't used to, turned her ankle when she tried to sidestep a small puddle. I doubt she would have yelped any louder if someone had dropped a frog down her dress. Her future husband, who had been looking the other way, turned around and grabbed her arm as she was going down. Thankfully, he kept her from landing on her face in the mud. But he wasn't quick enough to save her dress. By the time she regained her balance and stepped clear of the mire, there were several splashes of brown on the glossy white fabric.

At this point, let me just say that you've never seen panic until you've seen a bride get mud on her dress an hour before her wedding. The poor girl burst into tears as her attendants rushed to her side. Chaos reigned as they all talked at the same time, some consoling her and others offering frantic suggestions. Finally, they whisked her inside to the ladies' room where they soaped and rinsed the dirty spots as well as they could and held the fabric under a hand dryer. Later, when she walked down the aisle, the stains were less conspicuous, but still visible.

Unfortunately, that young woman is not the only mud-splattered bride I've known. The other is the church, the bride of Christ. You may remember that John the Baptist called Jesus "the bridegroom" (John 3:29 NLT), and that Paul said marriage is "an illustration of the way Christ and the church are one" (Ephesians 5:32 NLT). In Revelation 21:9, the church is specifically called "the bride, the wife of the Lamb" (NLT), and in Revelation 19:7–8, we even have a reference to their wedding reception:

"Let us be glad and rejoice and honor him. For the time has come for the wedding feast of the Lamb, and his bride has prepared herself. She is permitted to wear the finest white linen." (Fine linen represents the good deeds done by the people of God.) (NLT)

It's those last two sentences that spark my imagination.

I read recently about a movie star's wedding dress that cost more than three million dollars, and another that set a new world record with a 515-foot train. No doubt those were impressive gowns. But if, as this passage says, the church's wedding dress is made of the accumulated good deeds she has performed throughout history, surely hers is the most sparkling and beautiful of them all.

Imagine, then, how upset the Lord must be when we sling mud on her. Consider how it must break His heart when we thoughtlessly besmirch the one He gave His life for with unbecoming words and actions. And think about how angry it must make Him when we do it again and again.

We fully expect the world to throw mud on the bride of Christ. Those who resent what the church stands for will never grow tired of castigating her. But it's beyond tragic that God's own people would be caught doing it. And we are, more often than you might think.

MEET THE MUDSLINGERS

I've observed that four types of believers are responsible for most of the mud splatters on the bride of Christ.

The Missing

Group number one would be the *missing*. Every church in the world has some members who have gone AWOL. They are the people who, for whatever reason, have left the church. They haven't died or moved to another community. They've just stopped attending worship services and quit participating in activities. Sometimes they leave in a huff and other times they drift away gradually. But regardless of how they leave, sooner or later someone is going to notice and ask them why. At that point, they will have two choices: take responsibility or play the blame game. And if they choose the latter, you better duck because the mud is going to fly.

Awhile back, I talked to a couple of our AWOL members just a few days apart. The first gentleman engaged me in a lengthy conversation about his "frustrations" with our congregation, which, of course, were his reasons for dropping out. And, boy, did he have a long list of them! I sat and listened (and bit my tongue) while he hammered away. I remember thinking he couldn't possibly be talking about the same church I had been pastoring for the last seventeen years. Almost nothing he said connected with my experience. In fact, some of his criticisms were so silly that I got the feeling he was making them up as he went along. Or maybe he was parroting what he'd heard other people say about other churches. In the end, only one of his complaints rang true.

The second AWOL member I spoke to was a woman who didn't attack the church at all. She simply apologized for her laziness. She made no excuses, offered no rationalizations, and hurled no barbs. She assured me that she loved the church and acknowledged that she needed to start hauling her sorry self out of bed a little earlier on Sunday mornings. I really appreciated her honesty and told her so. It would have been very easy for her to try to take some heat off herself by doing what the man did.

Of course, I am not suggesting that churches are never guilty of driving people away. Everybody knows it happens. But we also know that every human being alive has a buck-passing gene that flares up every now and then. Since the beginning of time, people have been trying to deflect attention away from their own failures. Like Adam, who had the audacity to blame God for giving him the woman who enticed him to eat the forbidden fruit (see Genesis 3:12), the spiritually lazy can come up with some pretty outrageous (and groundless) accusations when they find themselves on the hot seat. And though they may not think about it at the time, those accusations stain the bride of Christ.

The Malcontents

The second group of mudslingers would be the *malcontents*. Back in the early 1980s, a series of *Saturday Night Live* skits featured Joe Piscopo and Robin Duke as Doug and Wendy Whiner. The Whiners moaned and complained constantly, even when something good happened to them. In one episode, their coach-class airline tickets were unexpectedly upgraded to first class, but they complained because the seats were too roomy and the bubbles from the complimentary champagne tickled their noses.

Sadly, there are Doug and Wendy clones in every church. They're the malcontents, the chronic complainers, the squeaky wheels that no amount of grease will ever silence. George Bernard Shaw once said that a drama critic is a person who leaves no turn unstoned. A church malcontent is a person who leaves no preacher or program unstoned. You can knock yourself out trying to make them happy (and a lot of preachers do), but it won't matter. They will still find something to complain about.

The good news is that such people tend to discredit and isolate themselves over time. Dealing with them is like rubbing up against sandpaper, and positive people quickly realize it and back away. The bad news is that they are still mudslinging machines even though they have few friends. At the bank, the barbershop, the beauty parlor, the grocery store, and a host of other places, they will spew their caustic comments and make the bride of Christ sound like a tramp to those who don't know her.

The Moochers

The third group of mudslingers would be the *moochers*. They're the people who have somehow gotten the idea that the church exists for the sole purpose of meeting *their* needs. Consequently, they suck up everything the church has to offer but rarely, if ever, give anything in return. They have what I call the "motel mentality." They walk in expecting everything to be perfectly prepared for their comfort and convenience, and walk out leaving the bed unmade and all their dirty towels piled up on the bathroom floor.

The problem, of course, is that the church isn't a motel. The members aren't guests, and the people on the church staff aren't maids and bellhops. On the contrary, in the biblical church, if anything, *everybody* is a maid or a bellhop. We're *all* supposed to be serving *one another*!

In John 13, Jesus washed His disciples' feet. When He finished He made a statement that forever put to rest the notion that we come into the church to be served. He said, "And since I, the Lord and Teacher, have washed your feet, you ought to wash each other's feet. I have given you an example to follow. Do as I have done to you" (John 13:14–15 NLT).

Nothing could be clearer, yet there are still people in every congregation who judge the church solely on the basis of the way it caters to their whims. And do they holler when it doesn't! Complaints and criticisms fly, and, once again, Christ's bride is splattered.

The Misbehavers

The fourth group of mudslingers would be the *misbehavers*. One of the best things about pastoring the same church for seventeen years is that you get to know so many people in the community. One of the worst things is that so many people get to know you. I often have people walk up to me at the mall, the supermarket, or in a restaurant and start talking to me as if we're old friends, even though I have no idea who they are. That's always a little disconcerting, especially when something they say knocks me off balance.

On one occasion, a woman I didn't know struck up a conversation with me in a local hardware store. Our discussion would have qualified as nothing more than idle chitchat if it hadn't taken this nasty turn:

Stranger: Doesn't _____ _____ go to your church?
Me: Yes, he does.
Stranger: Well, you should be very proud.
Me: Why is that?
Stranger: Because he was in our office yesterday and threw a fit.
Me: Really?
Stranger: Yes. Oh, he was real friendly at first and even invited me
　　　to church. Then, after his meeting with my boss, he was furious.
　　　He said a few choice words and even told my boss to go to hell
　　　as he was walking out the door.

7

I cringed. And apologized. And said something to the effect that occasionally good people do things they later regret. I assured her that our church would never condone such behavior and then, feeling like an idiot, said that I hoped she would still come and worship with us sometime. She never has, as far as I know.

Ah, those misbehavers!

They don't just sling mud on the bride of Christ. They pick up handfuls of it and smear it all over her. And then they haul off and punch her in the nose for good measure. It's my belief that no one does more to make the church look like a bunch of hypocrites than the misbehavers. The missing, the malcontents, and the moochers all put together probably don't do as much damage to the kingdom.

Years ago I heard a powerful quote. I've long since forgotten who said it, but it surfaces in my mind every time a misbehaving brother or sister makes headlines:

He that gives good advice, builds with one hand. He that gives good advice and sets a good example, builds with both hands. But he that gives good advice and sets a bad example, builds with one hand and tears down with the other.

John 13 offers us a great way to ensure that we're building with both hands. Jesus was spending His final hours with His disciples, which made it a very emotional time. They'd been through a lot together and were no doubt closer to one another at that point than they were to their own families. The very notion that something bad might be about to happen to Jesus was a heavy burden, but it was made even heavier by this nuclear bomb Jesus dropped into their conversation:

The Scriptures declare, "The one who shares my food has turned against me," and this will soon come true . . . The truth is, one of you will betray me! (John 13:18, 21 NLT)

This comment jolted the disciples. Whispers erupted as they tried to make some sense of it. Jesus couldn't possibly mean that one of them was a traitor, could He? But they knew He would never make such a statement if He didn't mean it. Finally, Peter nodded to John, who happened to be sitting next to Jesus, prompting him to lean over and whisper into Jesus' ear, "Lord, who is it?"

Right now, I hope this is your earnest prayer. In fact, I hope it will be your prayer as you move from chapter to chapter in this book. Please don't assume that when I identify blundering believers, I must be talking about someone else. Have the courage to ask, "Lord, who is it? Am I the one who does these things?"

Again, guilt in these areas doesn't necessarily mean you're a terrible person. It doesn't mean you don't love the Lord. It doesn't mean you aren't going to heaven. It could simply mean that you've slipped into some bad habits. The important thing is to recognize the seriousness of the problem, and one way to do that is to think about the damage that's being done.

THE DEVASTATING RESULTS
OF MUDSLINGING

There's no way to measure how much damage is done to the kingdom when believers thoughtlessly sling mud on the bride of Christ, but I suspect it's more than we realize. At the very least, we can safely make the following three statements:

FIRST, WHEN MUD IS SLUNG, THE DEVIL IS HANDED AN OPPORTUNITY. In Ephesians 6:12, Paul said, "For we are not fighting against people made of flesh and blood, but against the evil rulers and authorities of the unseen world, against those mighty powers of darkness who rule this world, and against wicked spirits in the heavenly realms" (NLT).

When I read that passage, I can't help picturing Satan as a military commander, pacing back and forth in a hi-tech control room. Banks of computers are gathering data from all around the world. Slimy creatures are hunched over computer keyboards, gathering and processing information. Suddenly, a siren begins to screech as one of them cries out, "We have a snide remark just confirmed!" Satan's ugly head snaps around as the name of the speaker and the exact location on planet Earth are reported. "Bravo, Team Six, let's do it!" he shouts and dispatches a team of snide-remark specialists to the scene with orders to get as much mileage out of the comment as possible.

That scene, though fictitious, may not be as far from reality as you think. I believe that if we had any idea how the unseen forces of evil mobilize and try to exploit our negative words and actions, we'd be a lot more careful. There's no doubt in my mind that Satan's favorite believers are the *missing*, the *malcontents*, the *moochers*, and the *misbehavers*—for the simple reason that they create endless opportunities for him to make the church look bad.

SECOND, WHEN MUD IS SLUNG, THE LOST ARE HANDED AN EXCUSE. I know a man who resisted Christ for several years. His wife and children were Christians, and he seemed to have no particular aversion to attending church. I would see him there about half the time. He even participated in some of our activities with his family. But he always balked when I or anyone else tried to talk to him about accepting Jesus as his Savior.

Then one day he did it.

There was no warning, no fanfare, and no hesitation. He just walked forward one Sunday morning at invitation time, committed his life to Christ, and was baptized. He even caught his wife off guard. When I asked him why he suddenly changed his mind, he gave a telling answer. He said, "I guess I just ran out of excuses."

I've never forgotten that incident and have used it many times to illustrate what I think is a powerful point. Some lost people will exhaust every excuse before they finally accept Christ. They're like the four-year-old boy who doesn't want to go to sleep. He needs a drink of water, has a tummy ache, hears a strange noise, has a headache, needs to go to the bathroom, and on and on until his parents are wondering what it was about having kids that ever made them think they'd like it. But then, just before they agree to put him up for adoption . . . silence! The little guy has run out of excuses. He's lost his will to keep up the fight. More important, he's grown so tired that sleep suddenly seems like a good thing.

Whether we like it or not (or even understand it), this is just the kind of process a lot of lost people go through before they accept the Lord. How disheartening it is to realize that we actually furnish them with excuses when we sling mud on the bride of Christ. Every splatter gives them yet another opportunity to rationalize and pushes them ever closer to a Christless eternity.

FINALLY, WHEN MUD IS SLUNG, THE LORD IS HANDED A HEARTACHE. When I was in my twenties and early thirties, I enjoyed coaching Little League. One evening, some parents were sitting in the stands during one of our games, ripping me apart. They thought I had the wrong kid pitching, the wrong kid batting leadoff, the wrong kid batting cleanup, and so on. (Of course, they were really just mad because I hadn't chosen *their* kids for those positions!) At any rate, the game didn't go well. We fell further and further behind and, as we did, the parents grew more and more unhappy. Our eventual drubbing only confirmed in their minds that I was a complete idiot and knew nothing about baseball and knew absolutely nothing about managing a baseball team.

But here's the kicker.

They didn't know my wife and, therefore, didn't realize she was sitting a few feet away.

She sat there throughout the entire game and listened to them criticize and mock me. Afterward, on the way home, she was completely distraught and told me everything she'd heard. When I asked why she didn't just get up and move to another section of the bleachers, she said she couldn't. She wanted to know what they were saying, even though it was killing her.

It's always tough to listen to someone bash your spouse. America's first lady, Laura Bush, has been quoted as saying that the hardest thing about being a politician's wife is having to listen to the ugly things people say about your husband—things you know are not true. And if we feel that way about our spouses, can't we assume the Lord would feel the same about His? Listening to people callously ripping His bride must break His heart, especially when the ripping is being done by people who ought to know better.

THE BIG QUESTIONS

Right now, the question you need to be asking is *not* whether you've ever slung mud on the bride of Christ. I'm sure you have. Just as I have, and every other Christian I know has. We've all had weak moments and bad days. We've all said and done things that reflected poorly on the Lord and His church. No, the question you need to be asking is whether you sling mud as a matter of habit or routine. That's really the critical issue. And it may be a tougher question to answer than you think.

Years ago, I knew a man who peppered his speech with profanity. It embarrassed his wife, who was a new Christian, so she began pressuring him to break the habit. He never denied that he had a tendency to let a bad word fly every now and then, but he honestly felt she was overreacting. He said his language wasn't nearly as bad as she made it out to be.

So she secretly recorded one of their conversations. She felt guilty doing it, but she knew it was the only way to convince him that he had a serious problem. And it worked. Before she played the tape, she asked him to estimate how many swearwords he had used. He guessed three or four. But when they replayed the tape, they counted a dozen. His swearing had become such a habit that his ears were becoming deaf to it.

Right now, I'm wondering if the same thing has happened to you. Have you been slinging mud on the bride of Christ for so long that you don't even realize you're doing it? Could it be that the people around you routinely cringe at your insensitive comments and questionable lifestyle choices, while you skip merrily along, oblivious to the effect you're having? Is it possible that you have become more of a hindrance than a help to your church?

As I said, this is a tough question to answer. It's so terribly hard to see ourselves as we really are. So I want to offer you some help. I'm going to ask four questions that will serve as a spiritual mirror for you . . . if you can find the courage to answer them honestly.

QUESTION #1: WHEN YOU HAVE A PROBLEM WITH YOUR CHURCH, DO YOU APPROACH YOUR LEADERS, OR DO YOU JUST START BLABBING ABOUT IT TO ANYONE WHO WILL LISTEN? Every church has some sort of leadership team: a pastor, elders, deacons, etc. There is a chain of command that exists for the very purpose of solving problems and keeping the church vibrant and healthy. Most church leaders are happy to hear about the members' concerns and to address them. Of course, some complaints are not legitimate and some problems are not fixable. But when they are, the majority of church leaders will act in good faith.

Yet, many unhappy church members never go to the leadership with their complaints. Amazingly, they never do the one thing that offers them the best chance of finding satisfaction. Instead, they immediately start venting their frustrations to their friends and neighbors and coworkers—all the people who *aren't* in a position to help, but certainly *are* in a position to fan the flames and spread those criticisms throughout the community.

What about you? Have you ever made an appointment to talk to your pastor or your elders about a complaint? Have you ever given them the courtesy of hearing about it and having a chance to deal with it *before* you began spreading it throughout the community? If not, let me encourage you to do just that.

If a complaint is boiling inside you right now, go to the person on your church's leadership team whom you feel the most connected to and share your thoughts in a calm and courteous manner. Then listen with an open mind. It's very likely that the leader you're talking to will have a perspective on the situation you haven't thought of or information you aren't aware of. It's absolutely critical that you be ready to process new information because you're probably going to get some. But whether you do or not, be ready to show some patience. Few problems are solved overnight, so you must be willing to give your leaders time to think, pray, and act. And while they're thinking, praying, and acting, keep quiet!

QUESTION #2: WHAT IS YOUR CHURCH CONTENTMENT QUOTIENT? This is a little mathematical equation I came up with that can be very revealing. Simply subtract the number of communities you've lived in from the number of churches you've attended. For example, if you've lived in the same community for the last ten years, but have attended three different churches, then your Church Contentment Quotient would be 2 for that period.

Obviously, the perfect CCQ would be 0. It would mean you've attended the same church for the entire time you've lived in your community. It would also likely indicate that you're not a malcontent. Malcontents generally have high CCQ's. I know one fellow who's worked his way up to a 4! He's lived at the same address since I've known him, but he's currently attending his fifth church! The church where I preach was number three. (Yes, he got upset with us and marched out the door slinging mud right and left.) Recently, I spoke to the pastor of the man's current church. Imagine my shock when I learned that he's now upset with them!

Of course, there are good reasons for changing churches. If the Word of God is compromised or people are mistreated, you'd probably be making a mistake if you *didn't* move on to a different congregation. But let's face it. People who bounce from church to church every couple of years simply because they get bent out of shape are generally malcontents. And, as we've already seen, malcontent is just another name for mudslinger.

So do the math. What's your CCQ?

QUESTION #3: DO YOU HAVE ANY HABITS OR ENJOY ANY ACTIVITIES THAT YOU WOULD HATE FOR YOUR CHURCH LEADERS TO FIND OUT ABOUT? Recently, I went into a local Italian restaurant to buy a gift card for a friend. The hostess at the front door directed me to the bar because the bartender was designated to handle all gift card transactions. I wasn't crazy about bellying up to the bar, even if it was just for a gift card. But since that particular restaurant is one of my friend's favorites, I set out in that direction.

I wish I hadn't.

Sitting at the bar with both hands wrapped around a half-empty mug of beer was someone I knew from church. I could tell he was deeply embarrassed when he looked up and saw me standing there. I said hello and tried to act as though it were no big deal, but he had been a Christian long enough to know it was. He even mumbled something about getting busted. It was one of those awkward situations that all preachers hate, but that we blindly walk into from time to time.

Again, what about you? Could you have been the guy on that barstool? Is there something going on in your life that you would be embarrassed for your pastor or other church friends to find out about? Are there times when your behavior simply doesn't square with your profession of faith?

If so, you are taking an awful risk. What's hidden in some dark corner of your life at this moment could be exposed to the whole world before the sun rises tomorrow morning. You may think it could never happen. You may have worked hard to design and construct a foolproof system for indulging your guilty pleasure on the sly. But trust me. There are millions of people walking around who will be happy to tell you all about how their own supposedly foolproof systems collapsed on them like a Chicago Cubs pennant drive. My guess is that yours will, too, sooner or later. And when it does, you will have soiled a whole lot more than just your own reputation. You will have muddied the bride of Christ.

QUESTION #4: HOW LONG HAS IT BEEN SINCE YOU BRAGGED ABOUT YOUR CHURCH? I know bragging isn't generally thought of as a virtue. But in this case I think we have an exception to the rule. In a world where mud is slung at the least provocation, there's just something refreshing about hearing someone speak in glowing terms about his church.

Several years ago, the teacher of one of our children's classes asked her students to finish the sentence "I love my church because . . ." Then she encouraged them to put their sentences on colorful posters that could be used to decorate their classroom. I was alone one day when I walked around the room looking at them. Before I finished, I found myself both grinning and getting a little misty-eyed. Here are some examples of the children's completed sentences:

□ "I love my church because Jesus lives there."

□ "I love my church because nobody here yells at me."

□ "I love my church because I love being with my friends."

□ "I love my church because my teacher is nice."

□ "I love my church because my little brother is in a different class."

After our Wednesday evening services, I often walk through the education area of our building. I stick my head into classrooms, greet the teachers, and talk to some of the children. It never ceases to amaze me how much joy and positive energy is in the air. Everywhere I turn I see smiles and hear giggles. I get waves and hugs and high fives. It's truly one of the highlights of my week.

But it makes me wonder.

Why do so many of us start out as children loving the bride of Christ so much, and end up just a few years later slinging mud on her? How is it that we can skip merrily through the halls singing "Jesus Loves Me" when we're eight, but by the time we're thirty-eight, all we can think about is how somebody in the youth department ought to keep those noisy brats quiet?

I don't know.

What I *do* know is that it's wonderful to hear someone brag about his church. How long has it been since you did?

I realize that if you've answered these questions honestly, you may now be feeling like a heel. You may be staring at your hands in horror, seeing mud stains for the first time. You may be digging at the grime under your fingernails and wondering how in the world you're ever going to get rid of it.

To answer that question, let me take you to the book of Job.

Throughout most of the book of Job, God keeps quiet and lets Job and his friends do all the talking. Or shall I say, the complaining. At one point, Job is so distraught that he starts slinging some serious mud. He says, "I cry to you, O God, but you don't answer me. I stand before you, and you don't bother to look. You have become cruel toward me. You persecute me with your great power" (30:20–21 NLT). But in chapter 38, God breaks His silence with an amazing speech that includes a penetrating question aimed right at Job. He ultimately says, "You are God's critic, but do you have the answers?" (40:2 NLT).

Ouch.

That had to sting.

Yet, to Job's everlasting credit, he offers the perfect response. He says, "I am nothing—how could I ever find the answers? I will put my hand over my mouth in silence. I have said too much already. I have nothing more to say" (40:4–5 NLT).

Something tells me that the question God asked Job is awfully close to the one He would ask of mudslingers everywhere: "You're the church's critic. You have no trouble enumerating her problems. But do you have the answers?"

Further, I have a feeling that the only appropriate response a mudslinger could ever offer is the one Job gave: "I'm sorry. I've said too much. I'll keep my mouth shut from now on."

An answer like that can come only from an enlightened, repentant heart. When you can offer it and really mean it, you will have taken the first step toward your new life as a recovering mudslinger.

Winning People to the Church Rather Than to the LORD

Let us fix our eyes on Jesus, the author and perfecter of our faith.
—HEBREWS 12:2 (NIV)

Do you ever wonder why so many people drop out of church? They do, you know.

In huge numbers.

The other day I had lunch with a well-known pastor I'd never met before. In the course of our conversation, I asked him how large his congregation was. When he said, "About four thousand," I was surprised. I'd seen the church's facility, and it didn't look nearly large enough to hold that many people, even in multiple services. When I made a comment to that effect, he quickly said, "Oh, I didn't mean we have four thousand in attendance. I meant

21

we have four thousand *members*." He went on to explain that they have only about fifteen hundred attendees on an average Sunday.

Sound familiar?

I'm guessing it does.

Practically every church in the world has an average weekly attendance that's less than its membership. Usually a lot less. And you can trust me when I tell you that the disparity isn't just the result of people being left on the membership roll after they've kicked the bucket or moved away. More than anything, it's the result of people drifting away or dropping out after losing interest, growing frustrated, or getting hurt.

Imagine what would happen if we were totally honest about this in our promotional materials. Perhaps our newspaper ads would bear the following headlines:

- ☐ There's only a fifty-fifty chance you'll survive your first year at our church, but we'd love for you to give us a try anyway!
- ☐ Our church is great! Just ask the 40 percent of our members who haven't left yet!
- ☐ Don't let all of our disgruntled former members fool you. We really are a very friendly congregation!

This is the church's embarrassing little secret . . . the one topic of conversation that is guaranteed to make a preacher blush and stammer. I know, because that's the effect it has on me. When I hear people start talking about all the folks who used to attend our church but have long since vanished, I've been known to quickly bring up last night's ball scores. Or maybe the latest trends in the Dow Jones Industrials.

But it's high time we stopped dancing around this subject. The church has a problem, and we desperately need to face it.

And fix it.

THE PROBLEM

We should never be surprised when there are defections among the Lord's followers. Nor should we panic. After all, Jesus Himself didn't have a 100 percent retention rate. In fact, though we don't know what His retention rate was, it doesn't appear to have been very good at all. John 6:66 says, "At this point many of his disciples turned away and deserted him" (NLT). That statement becomes even more stunning when you stop to realize that the defections started shortly after Jesus miraculously fed the five thousand and walked on water.

Talk about a tough audience!

And nothing much has changed. Disciples are still packing up and heading for the hills. What's tragic is that, in some cases, it's our fault. No, we can't be held responsible for those who were never serious in the first place, had ulterior motives, or simply decided that their old life was more fun. But we must take responsibility for the many people who became disillusioned because we misled them into thinking that the church would be the answer to all their problems—that it would save them, transform their lives, and meet all their needs. Imagine the crushing disappointment of a person who comes charging into the church full of enthusiasm, thinking that he's finally found the secret of happiness, only to be confronted with many of the same interpersonal conflicts, negative attitudes, and petty rivalries that he was trying to escape. *Anyone* would be tempted to defect under those circumstances!

Now, I realize you're probably squaring up your shoulders and saying, "But, Mark, I've never done what you're talking about! Never in my life have I misrepresented or overrepresented the church!"

Are you sure?

I mentioned in the last chapter that not nearly enough Christians brag on their churches. But among those who do, there is an undeniable tendency to make the church sound like it, rather than Jesus, is the source of their salvation. These happy, well-intentioned churchgoers love to tell people what a great pastor they have. They love to brag to their music-loving friends about the worship team or the concert choir. They love to tell their neighbors and coworkers who have little kids what a great children's ministry their church has. They talk endlessly about all the wonderful friends they've made in their small group. They rave about the Easter pageant and the living Christmas tree. And they beg their sports-loving friends to get involved in the softball program or the basketball league that has proved to be so much fun.

And that's just for starters.

After singing the church's praises, they then transition into a personal testimony that sounds eerily like a late-night infomercial:

> I can't believe how much my life has changed since I started going to church. For years I had the idea that church was boring, but boy, was I wrong! I've learned so much from our pastor, and I've made some wonderful new friends. Everybody who knows me says I've changed dramatically. All I know is, I'm much happier than I've ever

been in my life. I wish I had gone to church a long time ago! Won't you come and go with me?

Are you starting to see the problem?

It's possible for us to witness to our friends and get them all fired up and started to church without ever mentioning Jesus. The result is that they're won to the church rather than the Lord. They come into the body with all kinds of false assumptions and unrealistic expectations. They begin their faith experience with their hopes and dreams pinned on a group of imperfect people rather than the Lord of the universe. How can they help but be disappointed? How can we be surprised when they leave?

WHAT PEOPLE NEED TO KNOW
ABOUT THE CHURCH

Yesterday, I stopped at our local pharmacy to pick up a prescription. Because it was something I'd never taken before, I paused a moment to read the computer printout that itemized the drug's potential side effects. Constipation, which I have had and survived, was near the top of the list. But farther down were blurred vision, nausea, dizziness, tremors, and even internal bleeding. You've really got to hand it to those drug companies. They sure know how to comfort and encourage the sick!

On the other hand, it's good to know when there are hidden dangers. It's good to go into every situation with your eyes open, whether you're starting a new medication or starting to church. In fact, I've often wondered if churches ought to take a cue from the drug companies and provide a computer printout listing the dangers new church attendees should be on the lookout for. At the very least, I believe there are two warnings every person who's thinking about starting to church ought to be given.

WARNING #1: YOU WILL ENCOUNTER SOME DIFFICULT AND UNPLEASANT PEOPLE. I frequently say that I've met some of the greatest people in the world in church. What I rarely say (but what is just as true) is that I've also met some of the weirdest, most irritating people in church.

Many years ago, one of our church members stopped by my office just as I was getting ready to head home. He told me that his wife had thrown him out of the house, and he needed a place to spend the night. He begged me to let him sleep on the floor in our building for just one night. He promised he would be up and gone early in the morning and that I'd never know he'd been there. I knew the man had lots of problems and probably deserved to be kicked out of his house, but he was on foot, it was cold outside, and I didn't want him roaming the streets all night. Or worse yet, sleeping under a bridge. So I put him up in a classroom and told him to be gone by 8:00 a.m.

At 8:15 the following morning, I entered the building and paused to listen. Everything was quiet and there were no lights on. I breathed a sigh of relief. It appeared that he had indeed gotten up and left. So I went to my office, fired up my computer, and got down to business.

About 8:25—five minutes before my secretary was to arrive—I heard a noise. Someone was in the hallway outside my office door.

I looked up and saw the man step into my office in his underwear. His potbelly was hanging over his boxer shorts, his hair looked like a bomb had detonated on top of his head, and he was yawning and rubbing sleep out of his eyes. He looked like a Buddha statue come to life. "Mornin'," he said, as cheerfully as if we were bumping into each other at the local Starbucks.

I flew out of my chair like a NASA rocket heading for orbit.

"What are you doing?" I demanded.

He wasn't the least bit perturbed.

"Man, I overslept. I didn't think I'd get any sleep at all on that hard floor. But you know, that carpet's pretty soft. I actually slept pretty good."

And then I heard the door.

My secretary was arriving.

I could only imagine what she would think if she stuck her head into my office to say good morning (as she did every day) and saw a man standing there in his underwear. I figured I had about thirty seconds to avoid a complete disaster, and I didn't waste a single one. I ordered the man to get out of sight and get dressed, and I did it in such a way that he . . . well, let's just say he probably hadn't moved that quickly in a good long time.

About ten minutes later he stepped back into my office, fully dressed, and informed me that he probably wouldn't need to sleep in the church building more than three or four more nights and that he'd try to get an alarm clock so he wouldn't oversleep again. Then he had the gall to ask if I had a spare key he could use. I must have been staring at him like he had an arrow through his head because he suddenly paused and said, "What's wrong?"

I took a deep breath.

As calmly as possible (and it took tremendous effort), I explained to him that we weren't running a hotel and that he would have to find another place to sleep. I encouraged him to go work things out with his wife or, failing that, to stay with a friend or rent a real motel room. After all, he was gainfully employed. The church had done him a favor, but now it was time for him to take responsibility for his situation.

And that's when he became indignant.

He actually began to lecture me about my lack of concern for people in need. What's the church for, he asked, if it can't help those who are going through hard times? If my blood pressure had been taken at that moment, it probably would have broken the gauge. I suppose you could have fried an egg on the back of my neck.

I've had many experiences over the years that were just as odd and irritating as that one. And the reason is because we welcome everyone into the church. We don't turn people away just because they're rude, obnoxious, selfish, or look like Buddha in their underwear. In fact, God's power has been known to completely transform such people, so there is even an element of anticipation when a difficult person comes into the family. I've often looked heavenward and said with a smirk, "I can't wait to see what You're going to do with this one, Father!"

But welcoming everyone into the church means that every personality type (no matter how irritating), every opinion (no matter how idiotic), every weakness (no matter how pathetic), every maturity level, every size of ego, and every form of baggage will be represented. Some people are shocked when they get their feelings hurt at church. Considering the odd assortment of people who make up the average congregation, I've always thought it would be a lot more shocking if they *didn't* get their feelings hurt!

Several years ago, I took a preacher friend of mine to see our new church building when it was under construction. I stopped my car in front of a sign that read "Hard Hat Area." I'd seen the sign a hundred times and hadn't thought a thing of it. But as we were walking past it, my friend quipped, "You know, every church in the world ought to have a sign like that in front of it . . . even after the construction is complete."

It was a clever comment, but our laughter was suppressed by the fact that we knew it was all too true. Difficult and unpleasant people make going to church a pretty dangerous business.

WARNING #2: THE CHURCH YOU JOIN IS NOT ALWAYS GOING TO BE LIKE IT IS TODAY. When I counsel a young man and a young woman who are planning to get married, I always talk to them about the changes they can expect. And I use myself as an example.

When Marilyn and I got married, I owned a thin, athletic body, batted leadoff on our church softball team, had a head full of dark brown hair, and didn't snore. Now, more than thirty years later, I have love handles, I bat seventh, the top of my head is as smooth as a baby's bottom, and Marilyn says that I occasionally snore (though I want the record to show that she has no evidence that would stand up in a court of law).

Anybody with two eyes (and Marilyn would say, two ears) knows that I have changed. However, she hasn't dumped me. In fact, she will tell you that she likes the current version of me better than the version she married. She says that the physical losses I have suffered have been more than offset by the spiritual gains I have made.

So change is inevitable, but nothing to be afraid of. I tell every young couple I counsel that if they continue to grow in the Lord and focus on the deeper issues of the soul, the loss of a little hair or the addition of a few pounds will seem insignificant.

And then one day it hit me.

I needed to be having the very same talk with the people who were planning to enter into a relationship with our church. They, too, are generally in love with what they see right in front of them and seldom stop to think that the church will probably look and feel very different in a few short years.

Think about it.

A person generally loves the *pastor* of the church he joins. But what happens if that pastor leaves and is replaced by someone with a completely different personality or philosophy of ministry?

A person generally loves the *music* of the church he joins. But what happens when his favorite songs are replaced with songs he's never heard before and doesn't like?

A person generally loves the *location* of the church he joins. But what happens when the congregation decides to buy property ten miles farther away from his home?

A person generally loves the *fellowship* of the church he joins. But what happens when factions arise and a fight breaks out?

I could go on, but you get the picture.

Even cozy, happy, little picture-postcard churches can experience some dramatic changes. And, of course, many of them will be good. But even good changes can seem bad if you aren't expecting them. So, like the wife who is awakened for the first time by her husband's snoring . . . or like the Christmas-shopping husband who suddenly realizes his wife's dress size has doubled since they got married . . . a church member needs to be able to process those changes and keep them in perspective.

Jesus brushed up against this idea in Matthew 9:17 when He said, "No one puts new wine into old wineskins. The old skins would burst from the pressure, spilling the wine and ruining the skins. New wine must be stored in new wineskins" (NLT). People, like wineskins, need to be flexible enough to accommodate new strategies, methods, and formats without blowing up. And it's more likely that they will be if we warn them to expect change when they first come into the church.

I realize that what I'm suggesting here might not sit well with some Christians. You might be thinking that if we're too honest with our prospects about the church's imperfections, we might scare them off. Well, keep in mind, I never said we should portray the church as a house of horrors. I simply believe we should follow the example of Jesus and warn would-be disciples that what they're getting into might not always be peaches and cream. Consider these striking words Jesus spoke that I'm sure thinned the ranks of His prospects:

Foxes have dens to live in, and birds have nests, but I, the Son of Man, have no home of my own, not even a place to lay my head. (Matthew 8:20 NLT)

Everyone will hate you because of your allegiance to me. (Mark 13:13 NLT)

Do you think I have come to bring peace to the earth? No, I have come to bring strife and division! From now on families will be split apart, three in favor of me, and two against—or the other way around. There will be a division between father and son, mother and daughter, mother-in-law and daughter-in-law. (Luke 12:51–53 NLT)

Do you remember what I told you? "A servant is not greater than the master." Since they persecuted me, naturally they will persecute you. (John 15:20 NLT)

Obviously, Jesus was a lot more concerned about being honest with people than He was about building up large numbers of followers. In fact, we shouldn't forget that near the end of His life, the number of His followers dwindled down to almost nothing, but He kept right on telling people the truth about His kingdom. It had to be hard for Him to watch people walk away. Perhaps He was tempted to beg them to stay or to lure them back in with some fancy promises. If so, it was a temptation He resisted. I believe Jesus knew He would have *fewer* disciples, but *better* disciples if He warned them of the dangers they would face.

WHAT PEOPLE NEED
TO KNOW ABOUT JESUS

As I've already pointed out, sometimes Jesus is little more than an afterthought in our witnessing. We talk about everything related to the church except the One who gave His life for it, brought it into existence, and sustains it.

Imagine how this must frustrate God and tickle the devil!

I believe the only hope we have of making real disciples whose faith and commitment will last beyond the first disappointment they encounter is to make Jesus the centerpiece of our testimony. The question is, what exactly should we be telling people about Him? I can think of nothing better than what Jesus told people about Himself. In John 14:6, He said, "I am the way, the truth, and the life" (NLT).

FIRST, PEOPLE NEED TO KNOW THAT JESUS, NOT THE CHURCH, IS THE WAY. I'll never forget the first time I drove a car that had a Global Positioning System. It was several years ago when they were still pretty rare. I was so impressed that I raved about it to all my friends. "Imagine the car knowing exactly where to go and actually telling you when to turn right or left!" I gushed. And then one day, a friend of mine casually pointed out that Christians have had that technology on a spiritual level for thousands of years. I hadn't thought of it, but instantly I knew he was right. Jesus is our GPS . . . our Global Positioning Savior!

He said so Himself in John 8:12: "If you follow me, you won't be stumbling through the darkness" (NLT). In other words, you won't be making wrong turns, ending up in dangerous places, wandering down dead-end roads, or getting lost. On the contrary, you will be blessed. John 12:26 says, "All those who want to be my disciples must come and follow me . . . *And if they follow me, the Father will honor them*" (NLT, emphasis added).

This becomes critical information when you stop to consider that most people who show up at church for the first time have lost their way and are looking for direction. They may walk in looking like a million bucks and giving every indication that they've got their act together, but that usually isn't the case. As a pastor, I generally find this out during the second or third conversation I have with them. The first conversation usually consists of introductory chitchat. But one of the next two conversations will often reveal the real reason why they've come.

Their marriage is in trouble.

Their kids are getting off track.

Their finances are in shambles.

No matter what the words are, they always translate into the same basic message: "We've lost our way. We thought we knew where we were going, but we realize now that we've gotten off track and we need help."

Right then and there, people need to hear about Jesus, not the church. They need to be told that Jesus has the answers they're looking for, not that the Monday night church softball team is in first place. They need to be told that Jesus battled the same temptations we struggle with and overcame them, not that the young mothers' group is having their monthly shopping outing a week from Thursday. They need to be told that Jesus will bear their burdens and forgive their sins, not that the worship team is looking for a lead singer. You see, the softball team, the young mothers' club, the worship team, and all the other programs and activities of the church aren't the way. They can help people along the way, but they aren't the way.

Jesus is the way.

SECOND, PEOPLE NEED TO KNOW THAT JESUS, NOT THE CHURCH, IS THE TRUTH. I'd love to tell you that the church is a place where you never have to worry about being lied to, but that just isn't true. In fact, lying is so common among religious people that we even have a special word to identify it: *hypocrisy.*

I read recently about a woman whose husband was going on a cross-country business trip. He seemed to be lamenting the fact, so she decided to surprise him by secretly buying her own plane ticket and showing up unannounced at his hotel. Imagine her surprise when her knock on his hotel room door was answered by an attractive divorcée from their church.

Church and hypocrisy have always gone together. In fact, you can trace the relationship all the way back to the fifth chapter of Acts where Ananias and Sapphira lied in an effort to make themselves look more spiritual than they really were. And let's face it: Lies that are told in church are especially painful. You can handle it when a car mechanic tries to sell you repair work you don't need, or when a campaigning politician makes promises you know he doesn't intend to keep. Big deal. But when a pastor stands up in the pulpit and preaches a dynamic sermon on the evils of adultery after having had sex the night before with the wife of one of the deacons, it can be spiritually devastating.

About three weeks before construction was completed on our new worship center, I received a call from a woman who refused to tell me her name. She said her drive to work took her past our property every day. She'd watched the building take shape and could tell it was about finished. She confessed that she was feeling an almost overpowering urge to come and worship with us when we moved in, but was terrified to do so. She explained that her last church experience five years earlier had ended in disaster. There had been a big scandal involving the pastor. She and the other members had been duped and were deeply hurt. She swore at the time that she'd never set foot in another church building as long as she lived. But now, our facility seemed to be calling out to her, urging her to try again. Her voice cracked as she told me her story. I could tell the poor woman's wounds were deep and that her conflicting feelings were tearing her in two. After a lengthy conversation, I asked her again to tell me her name and literally begged her to attend our grand opening services. She said she'd prefer to remain anonymous and that she wasn't sure she could ever find the courage to go to church again, but that she would try.

Three weeks later, during our first worship service in the new building, I preached a message about Jesus titled "The Way, the Truth, and the Life." When I came to the second point about Jesus being the truth, I told the congregation about the phone call and the intriguing conversation I'd had with the mystery woman. And then I said this:

I don't know if that lady is here this morning. But ma'am, if you are, I want to tell you that we are honored to have you with us. I know it was incredibly hard for you to come here today, but I'm thankful that you found the strength and the courage to break your vow never to step inside another church building as long as you live.

I can tell there's a deep longing in your heart . . . a longing for truth. What I want you to understand is that truth is not in this building, or in these people, or in me. Especially in me. I am not the truth. Jesus is the truth.

I am only here . . . we are only here because we have the same longing you do. In a world full of lies, we, too, are searching for truth. All I ask is that you not make the mistake of believing that we are the truth. If you do, you'll be headed for another disappointment. As fallen human beings, we can't live up to that. Only Jesus can. He and He alone is the truth.

After the service, a woman I'd never met approached me and said, "I am not the woman who called you, but I could have been.

When you were telling her story, you were also telling my story. It was uncanny. And I want to thank you for what you said, because you're right. I've learned the hard way that Jesus alone is the truth. I only wish I'd known it years ago."

I don't know if the mystery caller was in church that morning or if she has ever visited our church. Sometimes I wonder if she's long since become a part of our family and has just never revealed her identity. Just in case, I make it a point to mention often that Jesus is the truth. If she ever does show up, I really want her to know.

FINALLY, PEOPLE NEED TO KNOW THAT JESUS, NOT THE CHURCH, IS THE LIFE. I'm sure you've heard it said that life begins at forty. Most teenagers think life begins when you get your driver's license. A romantic would probably say life begins when you meet your soul mate. But God would say that life begins when you finally come to realize that Jesus is the way and the truth.

Maybe you've never thought about it before, but there's significance to the order of the words *way, truth,* and *life.* Jesus listed *life* last because you don't get *it* until you first start following the *way* and believing the *truth.* The abundant life that He spoke about in John 10:10 is clearly the result of steadfastly following the way and sincerely believing the truth. It follows, then, that any person who isn't following the way and doesn't believe the truth isn't really living, at least not by God's definition. He's only existing.

We see it every day, don't we?

Look around (or perhaps in a mirror), and you'll see people who have no life. Oh, yes, they exist. They have kids, jobs, bills, schedules, obligations, problems, aches, pains, and stress, but they have no life. They have no energy. They have no passion. They have no fun. And worst of all, they have little hope of *ever* having any. On their current track, they have nothing to look forward to except more pressure and chaos.

The humorist Dave Barry talks about a time when he was really stressed out and needed a vacation. Completely bedraggled, he sat down to do some Internet research and ended up booking a reservation at a beautiful resort. When it was time to leave, he loaded up his laptop, cell phone, and briefcase. He corralled his kids and their toys, plus the dog, and then crammed five large suitcases into the family vehicle. When everything was loaded and he stood there wheezing from exhaustion, he realized there wasn't enough room left in the car for even a postage stamp.

And that's when it hit him like a piano dropped from a twenty-story building.

"What am I doing?" he said. "These are all the reasons why I need a vacation in the first place, and here I am taking them with me!"

Week after week, people who are burned out, stressed out, and worn out come staggering into our churches. The *last* thing they need is to be told about yet another church activity that needs to be squeezed into their already overcrowded schedules. Instead, they need to be told about Jesus' marvelous promise: "Come to me, all of you who are weary and carry heavy burdens, and I will give you rest. Take my yoke upon you. Let me teach you, because I am humble and gentle, and you will find rest for your souls. For my yoke fits perfectly, and the burden I give you is light" (Matthew 11:28–30 NLT).

Soul Rest.

To me, those two words are the perfect definition of the abundant life—the perfect description of what happens when you steadfastly follow in Jesus' footsteps and sincerely believe His truth. You suddenly have the ability to get up in the morning and face whatever monsters are waiting for you, while maintaining a peaceful, positive outlook. You find that you can go through your day with the calm assurance that things are in good hands and that there's nothing to worry about. In short, you experience the difference between living and existing . . . between thriving and surviving.

Not because of the church, but because of Jesus.

He alone is the way, the truth, and—*praise God!*—the life we've all been looking for!

By now, I hope I've convinced you that our witnessing needs to be Christ-centered and not church-centered. And I hope I've done it without diminishing your love and appreciation for the church. To make sure, let me share one more story. I think it will put everything I've written into perspective and lay the subject to rest.

In the 1500s, a huge chunk of marble was discovered near Florence. As news of the discovery spread, sculptors from every nearby village started showing up and begging for the opportunity to turn it into a magnificent statue. But the challenge proved greater than any of them could have imagined. One by one they gave it their best effort; each one chiseling, chipping, and scraping for days at a time. But they all walked away with their heads hung, defeated by the difficulty of working on such a gigantic piece of rock. Finally, the city fathers decided to contact Michelangelo. They believed if anyone could make something out of the boulder, he could.

The first thing he did was build a house around it so he could work in complete privacy. When the house was finished, he walked inside, shut the doors, and went to work. The townspeople passing by could hear the hammering and chiseling sounds coming from inside, but no one had any idea what the boulder was being turned into. Finally, after many months, the door swung open, and Michelangelo invited the world in to see what many people still believe is the greatest sculpture ever created: the statue of David.

My friend, there is a Master Sculptor who, when all others have failed, can take a shapeless, meaningless life and turn it into an object of startling beauty. And He, too, has built a house, a special environment in which to work. That house is the church. Many people come into it possessing no spiritual form or beauty and emerge sometime later completely transformed. But it isn't the house that brings about those changes, it's the Master Sculptor.

So, yes, it's good to invite people to church. Getting them into the Lord's preferred working environment is important. But let's make sure they understand where their hope lies. It's not in the house, but in the One who holds the hammer and chisel.

DUMB MOVE #3

Living Below the Level of Our Beliefs

It's always easier to fight for your principles than to live up to them.

—ADLAI STEVENSON

Their regular meeting place was a mall parking lot on the other side of the city from where they both lived. He would arrive just after dark and park his Toyota Highlander with the tinted windows as near as possible to a certain oak tree. A few minutes later, she would pull into a space on the same row but just a little farther from the mall, get out of her car, walk past his SUV, and continue on into a large department store. Once inside, she would play the part of the interested shopper, usually browsing through the shoes or the lingerie department because they were nearest the door. When the timing felt right, she would walk back out, stopping to climb into his vehicle before she reached her own. Then

41

came the kissing, the urgent groping, and the whispered words of passion. But tonight it would be different.

He'd called her cell phone while she was on her lunch break, hoping desperately that she'd be in a restaurant with some coworkers and unable to say much besides *yes* or *no* in a businesslike fashion. Instead, she was by herself, making a quick run to the dry cleaner's. He tried to keep his voice cheerful, but she immediately sensed something was up, probably because he called her by name instead of his usual term of endearment.

"What's wrong?" she asked.

"We need to talk."

"About what?"

"I'll tell you tonight."

"Why don't you tell me now?"

"Because I don't have time to get into it."

Silence.

"Is it bad news?" she asked.

"I guess that depends on how you look at it."

After another brief silence, she said, "You're going to dump me, aren't you?"

He winced. This was exactly what he'd hoped to avoid.

"Please, just meet me tonight so we can talk," he pleaded.

"What happened? Did your wife find out about us?"

"No, she didn't. Look, I have to go; just meet me tonight. Same place and time."

For a moment he thought she might have already hung up, but then she said, "I'll be there," and broke the connection.

Now it was seven hours later and he was parked in his usual spot, watching her get out of her car. Something told him she wouldn't bother to play out the shopping charade, and he was right. She marched straight to his vehicle and climbed in. After slamming the door harder than necessary, she sat and stared straight ahead with her hands pushed down deep into her jacket pockets. He could tell from the outline of the fabric that her hands were balled into fists, and he suddenly wondered if she would be using them on him before their conversation was over.

"Thanks for coming," he said softly.

She snapped her head around. "Why are you doing this?" she demanded. "Tell me why you're doing this."

At that point, he decided to chuck the speech he'd been rehearsing all afternoon in his mind. She'd known from the beginning what was coming, so there was no point in needlessly dragging things out by waxing philosophical.

"Because," he said, "this thing we're into . . . it isn't right."

Immediately, she was irate. "This *thing*? What do you mean '*thing*'? Are you by any chance talking about our *relationship*?"

He sighed. "Yes, I'm talking about our relationship. It isn't right, and we both know it. I'm married, for heaven's sake."

She looked at him incredulously and said, "So when did you suddenly get a conscience? Because, as I recall, you didn't have much of one last Thursday night at the Marriott. What's the matter? Did your pastor friend preach about the evils of adultery yesterday? Did he stand up and remind all you good little Christian boys that it's wrong to be getting some on the side? Is that it?"

That was indeed it, as a matter of fact. But he didn't want to go there. It was too painful. And besides, she wasn't a believer. He was sure she couldn't possibly understand the guilt he'd been feeling since he'd heard the pastor's sermon.

"Look," he said, "I was wrong. I was an idiot. All I can do is say I'm sorry and ask you to forgive me."

"Forgive you for what?" she asked, picking up a head of steam. "For flirting with me like some stupid schoolboy? For begging me to give you my cell phone number? For calling me every day until I agreed to go out with you? Or maybe you'd like me to forgive you for thinking up this idiotic parking lot game we have to play every time you get in the mood to fool around a little?"

Her words cut deep. Probably deeper than she intended, which was saying something. All he could do was stare slump-shouldered at the dash.

And then, suddenly, her tone of voice changed. The anger was gone, and he could tell she was weeping.

"Just answer me one question and then I'll go," she said. "Why? Why, if you think it's so wrong, did you do it?"

He felt a tear spill onto his cheek.

"I wish I knew."

Thankfully, the man who told me that story repented and, to my knowledge, never made the same mistake again. Nevertheless, for a period of four months he violated every moral conviction he'd ever held. He indulged in behavior he would have found reprehensible in anyone else. He said and did things he would have been horrified for any of his friends or loved ones to know about. Simply put, for those four months he lived far below the level of his beliefs.

Of course, you could say that since we're all sinners, we all live below the level of our beliefs. But that's not what I'm talking about.

As I said in the introduction of this book, I'm not concerned about the isolated mistakes that flow naturally out of our humanity. I'm not concerned about the times when our behavior *momentarily* dips below the level of our beliefs. As imperfect human beings, we're always going to have those moments when we can only slap our foreheads and say, "Duh!" Instead, I'm concerned about the sins we become blind to—the sins that become ingrained in our lives and that cause us to sink below the level of our beliefs and live there for extended periods of time. I'm talking about the harbored sins that cause God to wince in pain and Satan to giggle like a sixth grader with a whoopee cushion.

And notice, I said "sins," not sin. Even though I started this chapter with the example of a man who had an extramarital affair, I'm not suggesting that this blunder relates only to sexual sin. On the contrary, any kind of disobedience, if you become blind to it, can become like concrete shoes to your soul.

THE SINS THAT DRAG US DOWN

When a married man carries on a four-month affair, everyone— including him—knows it's wrong. But let me mention three sins that often slip past our spiritual radar and nestle unnoticed into our daily routines.

Materialism
The first would be *materialism*. Not long ago a female friend of mine told me an interesting story about how she discovered this sin in herself.

She was preparing a series of lessons for her Sunday school class on the subject of materialism and had what she thought was a brilliant idea. She would challenge her students to go home and walk through their houses, looking for evidence of materialism. She'd encourage them to look for any signs of excess, any indications that they bought things they didn't need or couldn't afford. She said that as she sat at her computer pecking away, she actually smiled and congratulated herself for coming up with such a great idea.

And then it hit her.

If she was going to ask her students to do this, shouldn't she do it herself? And what would she find if she did? Suddenly, it dawned on her that she would indeed find incriminating evidence, and she knew exactly where.

She got up from her desk, walked into her bedroom, and opened the door to her closet. There, she saw dozens of pairs of shoes. Some on racks, some still in the boxes, and several that she'd worn recently scattered about the floor. On a whim, she got down on her hands and knees and started counting. Ten minutes later, she sat on the carpet feeling thoroughly ashamed. She'd counted eighty-four pairs of shoes and ran across several that she'd never worn and had even forgotten she owned. And that's not to mention all the pairs that were almost exactly alike.

Suddenly, she was on a mission. She marched into the kitchen and grabbed a fistful of thirty-gallon trash bags, then ducked back into her closet and started sorting her shoes. By the time she was finished, she'd chosen fifty pairs—some never worn—that she would drop off at a local thrift store.

Let me encourage you to do what my friend did. Take an honest inventory of your life and see if you find any evidence of material-ism. Are you so deep in credit card debt that you need a snorkel to breathe? Are your closets and garage jam-packed with stuff you never use and can't even remember why you bought? Are you con-stantly buying the latest techno-gadget, not because you need it, but simply because it's cool? And, at the same time, do you find it difficult to tithe? Do you find spending money at the mall an exhilarating experience, but putting money into the offering plate a painful one?

Jesus said, "Wherever your treasure is, there your heart and thoughts will also be" (Matthew 6:21 NLT). Clearly, He's saying that our commitment to Him will rise and fall in direct propor-tion to our interest in material things. That's why Satan works so hard to tantalize us with toys and trinkets. He knows he can suck the power right out of the church if he can keep us distracted and preoccupied. In addition, he knows that for every dollar we spend on stuff that's ultimately going to burn, that's one dollar we won't be spending to reach an eternal soul for Christ.

My friend with the eighty-four pairs of shoes told me the thing that really bothered her about her shoe collection was that it rep-resented so much wasted money. Money that could have fed no telling how many starving children or reached no telling how many lost souls with the gospel.

There's no way to do the math, but just imagine if we could add up all the time, energy, and money Christian people waste on the pursuit of things they don't need and will probably never wear or use. The numbers would be mind-boggling and would no doubt explain why the church often seems so impotent.

And why the devil can't quit smiling.

Worry

The second sin that tends to slip under our spiritual radar is *worry*. Most Christians understand that worry is a sin. Philippians 4:6 says, "Don't worry about anything; instead, pray about everything" (NLT). Yet, we do worry. A lot. And I think I finally figured out why.

In 2004, we central Floridians saw the paths of three major hurricanes intersect right over our area. As the first one, a rather disagreeable chap by the name of Charley, was churning toward us, I took some precautions, but I wasn't really uptight. After all, we'd lived in Florida for fifteen years, and all the other hurricanes that had visited our area either missed us or fizzled out over the middle of the state, where we happen to live. I figured our biggest inconvenience might be that we'd lose power and I'd have to light some candles and run my laptop off the battery to work on my book.

I couldn't have been more wrong if I'd predicted a fifty-year marriage for Jennifer Lopez and Ben Affleck.

For forty-five minutes, our area was relentlessly pounded by 110-mile-an-hour winds. I live in a new concrete-block home, and I could literally feel the whole house trembling. And yes, in a storm of such power, it really does sound like a freight train is about to plow through your living room. I'd heard people say that for years, but I had no experience to verify it. Now I do.

Because the storm hit in the middle of the night and knocked out all power, we had to wait until the next morning to get out and assess the damage. And what we saw was breathtaking. Enormous trees were uprooted. Brick walls were lying on the ground in pieces. Metal road signs embedded in concrete were sheared off like someone had taken a saw to them. Power poles were snapped like toothpicks. Open fields were strewn with debris. I even saw an eighteen-wheeler that was tipped over on its side.

And that's not to mention the homes.

I felt nauseous as we drove through the neighborhoods of our community and checked on our friends. Roofs were gone. Walls were collapsed. Windows were shattered. Garages were missing. Vehicles were crushed under fallen tree trunks. And then, of course, there were the reports of the dead and injured that we were listening to as we drove.

That's when my whole attitude toward storms changed. Never before had I cared anything about the Weather Channel, but suddenly it was my favorite station. In two days, I knew the names of all the anchors and field reporters. Every time I heard the words *tropical depression*, I went into one. And about two weeks later when they told us another hurricane was on its way, I confess . . . I worried.

Here's my point.

The naive don't have much of a problem with worry. Young people, for example, who've never seen or experienced a terrible storm, tend not to be afraid of them. But anyone who's had the roof ripped off his house by a tornado or a category 4 hurricane will break out into a cold sweat when the weather service issues a warning. It seems logical to think that older people would worry less, but the opposite is usually true. We tend to worry more because we know from experience how cruel life can be.

Not long ago, I was teaching a class at our church that was primarily made up of middle-aged and senior adults. Out of curiosity, I made up a survey and asked them to take it anonymously.

One of the questions had to do with the sins they struggle with. I listed greed, gossip, worry, laziness, grumbling, pride, lust, and anger, and then provided a blank for them to fill in a sin that I might not have listed. They were to circle or write in the ones that gave them the most trouble. Interestingly, worry was the only sin that was circled on every paper.

The real problem with worry is not just that it ties your stomach up in knots and steals your joy. That certainly would be bad enough. But it also serves as a wrecking ball to your witness. It's a flashing neon sign you carry around with you . . . a sign that says, "Don't be fooled by my words; I really *don't* trust God to take care of me!"

I once read that Martin Luther was a worrier and often suffered through lengthy periods of depression. One morning he got up and found his wife moving about the house in a black funeral garment. Curtains were drawn and candles were lit as if the family were in mourning.

Alarmed, he asked, "Who died?"

His wife turned to him and said, "God did."

He said, "Don't be ridiculous! God didn't die!"

To which his wife responded, "Oh no? Then why have you been acting like it for the last week?"[1]

We may believe that God is alive, on His throne, and in control. But when we allow ourselves to worry, we're living below the level of that belief. We're sending the opposite message to the world and draining the power right out of our witness. No one is ever impressed with the kind of faith that collapses under pressure.

Or in the path of a hurricane.

Superiority

One more sin that we tend not to see in ourselves is what I call the sin of *superiority*. Jesus told a powerful story, recorded in Luke 18, about two men who showed up at the temple at the same time to pray. One was a Pharisee and the other was a crooked tax collector. The Pharisee stood by himself and prayed, "I thank you, God, that I am not a sinner like everyone else, especially like that tax collector over there! For I never cheat, I don't sin, I don't commit adultery, I fast twice a week, and I give you a tenth of my income" (vv. 11–12 NLT).

At the same time, the tax collector was on the other side of the room with his head down, beating his chest in sorrow, and praying, "O God, be merciful to me, for I am a sinner" (v. 13 NLT). Jesus then concluded by saying that in the final accounting, the crooked tax collector would be justified before God, and not the proud Pharisee, because in God's system the proud are humbled and the humble are exalted.

To be honest with you, I've never witnessed a display of pride quite as extreme as the example Jesus gave. But I do quite often see more subtle indications of a sense of superiority in God's people.

For example, recently I spoke at a men's gathering at a large church. I ended up sitting at a round table with seven other guys for dinner. I didn't know them, but they were your run-of-the-mill characters. As I recall, a couple were retired, one was a schoolteacher, another was a plumber, and so on. Throughout the meal, the conversation was quite pleasant, and I was enjoying it very much. But then someone brought up a situation that completely changed the mood. Apparently, someone they all knew—I assumed it was a fellow church member—had recently left his wife for another woman. As soon as his name was mentioned, those jovial, mild-mannered good ol' boys were suddenly transformed into spiritual pit bulls.

For the next several minutes, those guys piled on their fallen brother with some very harsh comments. One called him an idiot, while another said he must have rocks for brains. I said nothing, which is no doubt to my shame, but I couldn't help thinking how cocky those guys suddenly seemed, as if none of them had ever made a stupid mistake. I would have been willing to bet that if the histories of those guys could have been revealed at that moment, there would have been plenty for each of them to be embarrassed about.

But in the end, I couldn't really blame them because I knew I'd done the same thing a thousand times. I, too, have slipped into that cocky, superior attitude that causes me to throw out words of judgment and condemnation as easily as I might make a comment about the weather. And I, too, have a spiritual rap sheet . . . enough embarrassing failures on my record to completely disqualify me from ever judging someone else. But I do it anyway.

The incident reminded me of a comment author Steve Brown made. He was talking about our tendency to be arrogant, and he said, "Because grace runs down hill, it's very important that you not stake out your territory at the top of the hill."[2] But that's what we do. We march right to the top of the hill as though we own the place.

This, of course, is one of the biggest reasons why unbelievers hate us so much. They see us as pious, condescending snobs. We bristle when that accusation is made, but more often than we realize, that's just what we are.

ELEVATING OUR GAME

In sports, when a team is performing below the level of its talent, you'll hear the players say, "We need to elevate our game." I think it's high time we Christians realized that we need to elevate *our* game. We need to root out those sins that have settled comfortably into our daily routines, that diminish our joy, that drain the power out of our witness, and that keep God frustrated and the devil entertained. Let me suggest a couple of things we can do that will help us toward this goal.

Put the Power Back into Preaching

First, we can put the power back into our preaching. Since the days of the great Old Testament prophets, God has used preaching to call people to repentance. The city of Nineveh, for example, was called to repentance by Jonah, and 120,000 people responded (see Jonah 3:6–10; 4:11). And on the day of Pentecost, three thousand Jews responded to Peter's sermon by repenting and accepting Christ (see Acts 2:41). But even when masses of people don't respond, a sermon can still have a profound effect. At the beginning of this chapter, I told you about a man who was motivated to break off an illicit affair because of a powerful sermon his pastor preached. I don't think more than three people ever knew about his affair or his repentance. But his decision to elevate his behavior back to the level of his beliefs no doubt preempted a major catastrophe for himself, his family, and his church. There's just something about a great sermon that has a way of changing hearts and saving lives.

But I'm sensing a problem in this area.

Is it just me, or have you noticed that more and more preachers are sounding like talk-show psychologists? I was channel surfing the other night and came across a preacher who is currently riding a wave of popularity. He was speaking in a large auditorium. I suppose there must have been ten thousand people in the arena, hanging on his every word, taking notes, and laughing and applauding in all the right places. And his delivery was flawless. He used no notes, was witty and charming, and literally never stopped smiling. I instantly found myself admiring him.

But the longer I watched, the more uneasy I felt. First, he was talking about the physical and spiritual health benefits of laughter. Initially, I thought I just caught him in the middle of an illustration. But no, I quickly realized the entire focus of his message was laughter. The second thing I noticed was that he used almost no Scripture. One verse, to be exact, in the twenty minutes or so that I watched. Oh, he quoted plenty of experts, some of whom weren't Christians, but there was a striking absence of Scripture. Third, I noticed that he kept talking about happiness as if it were the supreme goal everyone ought to be shooting for. Not holiness. Not peace with God. Just happiness. And finally, I couldn't help noticing that he mentioned Jesus only once, in passing.

Now, I fully acknowledge that it's unfair to draw too many iron-clad conclusions from a twenty-minute sermon excerpt, but that's not the only such experience I've had. So many sermons I'm hearing nowadays are focused on fluffy, feel-good topics and steer clear of any talk about sin or personal responsibility. Jesus, it sometimes seems, has become just another "expert" to be quoted along with all the other authors and psychologists making the talk-show rounds. And heaven help the poor preacher who dares to stand up and boldly proclaim the gritty truth about sin and its consequences. In a flash, he'll be labeled fanatical, or worse, intolerant.

Could this be one of the reasons why our behavior has slipped below the level of our beliefs in so many areas? Have we become so obsessed with being seeker-friendly that we're reluctant to offer the whole counsel of God? I wonder what God must think when He sees so many preachers harping on those Bible verses that support their best-selling principles of success and happiness, while at the same time completely ignoring the passages that get tough on sin. Would He prefer that we spend more time teaching people how to be holy?

I can't help thinking about John the Baptist.

His preaching was exactly the opposite of what I'm talking about. Coming out of the wilderness in camel's hair clothing, he was about as unpolished as you could get. And he obviously didn't grasp the concept of being seeker-friendly. Instead of stroking people, he challenged them. He bluntly condemned immorality and hypocrisy, even when speaking to the most powerful political and religious leaders of his day. In fact, it appears that the theme of every sermon he preached was repentance (see Luke 3:3). Can you imagine anything so politically incorrect? Why, if a preacher nowadays stood up and railed against sin and called for repentance week after week, he'd have a hard time keeping a job.

Yet, Jesus Himself said that John the Baptist was more than a prophet. He was the greatest man who'd ever lived (see Luke 7:26–28). Clearly, He wouldn't have given John such a ringing endorsement if He'd disapproved of his preaching style. On the contrary, it appears to have been John's boldness that the Lord so deeply appreciated.

Now, don't get me wrong. I do know there are still a lot of great preachers out there who are preaching the whole counsel of God. And I'm certainly not suggesting that our preaching needs to be so hard-nosed that we leave people bruised and bleeding at the end of every service. But I do believe that a lot of our pulpit pros need to be injected with some of the spunk of John the Baptist. We need to remember that one of the primary reasons why God gave us the Bible in the first place was to help us "realize what is wrong in our lives" (2 Timothy 3:16 NLT). God help us if people can sit in our churches week after week, listening to sermon after sermon with smiles on their faces, and never realize that they're living below the level of their beliefs.

Move Your Heart Closer to the Lord

The second thing we can do to elevate our behavior back up to the level of our beliefs is to move our hearts closer to the Lord. Remember when David dipped below the level of his beliefs and ordered his soldiers to bring Bathsheba to his bedroom late one night? That fateful decision propelled him into a yearlong period of darkness in which he orchestrated a cover-up and murder plot that would have made Al Capone proud.

We can only assume that during that entire time, David was still worshipping as usual. Imagine him in a meeting with his generals, putting the finishing touches on a plot to murder Bathsheba's husband, and then realizing that it's time to hotfoot it over to the house of the Lord. "Let's hold that thought, fellas," he says. "It's time for our morning prayers. We'll pick up this discussion when we get back."

It seems unthinkable that such a thing could happen. But apparently it did, which only goes to show at that point in his life,

David's worship was nothing but a hollow ritual. He was showing up on time, warmly greeting all of his friends, singing all the most popular new psalms, and no doubt offering the kind of beautiful prayers you would expect from one of history's greatest poets. Then, when the service was over, he was walking unchanged right back into his pathetic, morally corrupt little life.

What was his problem? God tells us in Isaiah 29:13:

> These people say they are mine. They honor me with their lips, *but their hearts are far away.* And their worship of me amounts to nothing more than human laws learned by rote. (NLT, emphasis added)

One time I was teaching a class on worship and asked my students what was the most important thing a person could take to church. A preacher who happened to be in the class jokingly said, "His offering!" and everybody laughed. A couple of other people said, "A friend." But the majority agreed that a Bible would be the most important thing a person could take to church.

You can imagine, then, the blank stares I got when I announced that all of those answers were wrong. Before they could start to argue, I read Isaiah 29:13 and said, "Think about it. Your heart is the one thing you can't afford to be without when you come before God. If you leave your heart at home, everything you do here is an exercise in futility. Worse than that, it's an insult to God." Then I asked them to turn over to Amos 5:21–23, and we read the following words that God spoke to His people:

> I hate all your show and pretense—the hypocrisy of your religious festivals and solemn assemblies. I will not accept your burnt offerings

and grain offerings. I won't even notice all your choice peace offerings. Away with your hymns of praise! They are only noise to my ears. I will not listen to your music, no matter how lovely it is. (NLT)

Here's the bottom line: History proves that when powerful preaching and tender hearts come together in the presence of almighty God, incredible things always happen. Lives are changed. Families are changed. Churches are changed. Sometimes entire communities are changed. But when the meat of the gospel is replaced by spiritual junk food and the hearts of the worshippers are far away, then people will be able to go right on living, guilt-free, far below the level of their beliefs. Oh, yes, we can still draw big crowds and put on a great show on Sunday mornings. We can trot out a killer band, put on clever skits, show heartrending video clips, and offer slick, seeker-friendly messages. But as God Himself said, it will all be noise to His ears.

As I come to the end of this chapter, I want to reiterate that nobody's expecting you to be perfect, most of all God. Psalm 103:13–14 says, "The LORD is like a father to his children, tender and compassionate to those who fear him. For he understands how weak we are; he knows we are only dust" (NLT). God knows you're occasionally going to "slip and dip." That is, slip up and momentarily dip below the level of your beliefs. The real challenge is to not let sin settle in and make itself at home. If you do, it doesn't matter what else you bring to the table in terms of personality, intellect, or ability, you're going to be a hindrance to the kingdom. Speaking of hindrances to the kingdom, I love the story about the knight who returned to his castle just as the sun was setting. He was battered and beaten. His armor was dented, his helmet was crushed, he had blood all over his face, and his horse was limping with a broken leg. When the king saw him, he said, "What happened to you?"

"My lord, I have been courageously harassing your enemies to the west."

"My what?" the king replied. "I don't have any enemies to the west."

The knight thought for a moment and said, "You do now."

If you want to be a help to the kingdom and not a hindrance, make sure your behavior meets with the King's approval.

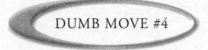

DUMB MOVE #4

Speaking Above the Level of Our Knowledge

He who knows little knows enough if he knows how to hold his tongue.

—ITALIAN PROVERB

Okay, boys and girls, it's time for a pop quiz. I'm going to make a series of statements, and you are to answer *true* or *false*.

Are you ready?

Here we go!

1. Bulls get angry when they see red.
2. James Cagney said, "You dirty rat."
3. Vikings wore helmets with horns on them.
4. Camels can go longer without water than any other animal.
5. Captain Kirk said, "Beam me up, Scotty."

6. S.O.S. stands for "save our ship."
7. The Great Wall of China can be seen from the moon.
8. The proper name for the British flag is the Union Jack.
9. Sherlock Holmes said, "Elementary, my dear Watson."
10. Charles Lindbergh was the first person to fly nonstop across the Atlantic.

Just for fun, I gave this little test to a friend of mine. He answered every question *true* and seemed puzzled that they were so easy. You can imagine his surprise, then, when I informed him that his grade was a big fat zero. All of the statements are false, according to the Bureau of Misinformation.[1]

So how did *you* do?

I'm guessing that your grade probably wouldn't put you on the dean's list, and that right about now you're all bristled up and ready to argue. After all, you've seen the Minnesota Vikings team logo often enough to know that Vikings had horns on their helmets. (The problem is, the guys who designed the logo went for style over historical accuracy.) And you've seen enough *Star Trek* episodes to know that Captain Kirk did indeed say, "Beam me up, Scotty." (Actually, it was "Beam me up, Mr. Scott.")

Isn't it amazing how much misinformation worms its way into our heads? Perhaps the eighteenth-century American philosopher William James had it right when he said, "There is nothing so absurd but if you repeat it often enough people will believe it."

Another good (and much more important) example would be the oft-quoted phrase "the separation of church and state." Most Americans would swear it's in the Constitution. We've heard it quoted so many times by politicians and TV commentators that the average person doesn't even question its legitimacy. Every time some wild-eyed activist regurgitates it in an effort to get a Nativity scene deleted from a school play or a monument removed from a courthouse lobby, Joe Good Ol' Boy just shrugs and figures the activist knows what he's talking about.

Yet neither the words nor the idea is in the Constitution. The words come instead from a letter Thomas Jefferson wrote to the Danbury Baptists in 1802. What's more, in a bitterly ironic twist, the purpose of the letter was not to warn the Baptists to keep their religious expressions and symbols out of the public arena, as some today would have us believe. It was—are you ready for this?—to reassure them that the government would never interfere with their practice of religion!

The point is, misinformation is constantly worming its way into our heads because people are constantly speaking above and beyond the level of their knowledge. And I'd love to tell you that unbelievers are the primary culprits. I'd love to say that this is one area where we Christians are relatively guilt-free—that we consistently keep our mouths shut until we get our facts straight. But I can't. In fact, I'm forced to admit that we're probably the worst offenders. And we have been for a long, long time.

For example, in Paul's first letter to Timothy, he addressed the problem as it was affecting the church in Ephesus. Speaking of certain teachers who were short on love and sound doctrine, he said, "They have turned away from these things and spend their time arguing and talking foolishness. They want to be known as teachers of the law of Moses, but they don't know what they are talking about, even though they seem so confident" (1 Timothy 1:6–7 NLT).

Paul tacked on that last phrase because he understood what I'm sure you've noticed: that people who don't have a clue what they're talking about never seem to lack confidence. A seasoned scholar will often speak humbly, acknowledging that the things he doesn't know far outnumber the things he does. But a fool will recklessly spew rumor, hearsay, and speculation like it's gospel. Maybe that's what Solomon meant when he said, "Being a fool makes you a blabbermouth" (Ecclesiastes 5:3 NLT).

THE SIN OF THE TONGUE
WE RARELY NOTICE

James 3:1–12 is a powerful passage about the damage an un-controlled tongue can do. The author practically rants on the subject, at one point even saying that the tongue is "full of wickedness that can ruin your whole life" (v. 6 NLT). And no one would disagree because the pages of history are loaded with corroborating evidence.

That's why we preach the passage with unbridled fervor. Thumb through any veteran preacher's sermon file, and you'll discover a whole stack of ripsnorters on gossip, rumormongering, criticism, and lying. But I dare say that the one sermon you won't find is the one about speaking above the level of your knowledge. It's the one sin of the tongue that consistently manages to escape notice. Why? Probably because it usually comes from a different kind of person. Liars, gossips, and caustic critics are always seen as troublemakers, while a person who speaks above the level of his knowledge is often a good-hearted soul with the best of intentions.

Let me give you an example.

Several years ago, I was the pastor of a sweet couple in their mid-twenties who had three children under the age of five. That young mom had her hands full on the best of days, but things really got dicey on one occasion when all three of the children came down with flu-like symptoms at the same time. Because her husband was out of town on business, we checked on her daily to make sure all of her needs were met. Usually her voice was light and cheerful, but one day when I called it sounded strained, as though she was upset about something. And then, not fifteen seconds into the conversation, she broke down and began to sob. I pleaded with her to tell me what was wrong, but she couldn't pull herself together enough to speak. So I hung up the phone, grabbed my wife, and raced over to her house.

What we learned when we arrived was that she'd had a visitor. A neighbor lady had dropped in to share what she called "a word from the Lord." The woman read the passage in Hebrews 12 that talks about the Lord's discipline, then proceeded to tell the young mother that the sickness afflicting her children was God's judgment on her for some sin in her life. Further, she virtually guaranteed that the children would not get well until the mom confessed her sin and got right with God.

One of the reasons the lady's words had such a devastating impact was because the young mother was a new Christian and not well-versed in the Scriptures. She was beginning to study her Bible, but hadn't yet read the Hebrews passage and found it truly frightening. Add to that the facts that she was already emotionally wrung out, physically exhausted, and worried sick about her children, and you can understand why she broke down. It took lots of counsel, some serious Bible study, and the recovery of her children to get the young woman out of her funk.

But now, let's think for a moment about that neighbor lady. She was the very picture of a confident Christian, just like the teachers Paul talked about. She marched into the young woman's house with her Bible tucked under her arm, a few pet verses highlighted in bright yellow ink, and a lecture all prepared. I can just imagine her speaking with the strident tone of a person who thinks she has all the answers, then walking out the door with a self-satisfied glow, congratulating herself on a job well done. But she was obviously speaking far above and beyond the level of her knowledge.

For one thing, she accused the young woman of harboring sin, when in fact she and her husband were growing in the faith and trying hard to bring their lifestyle more into line with God's Word. They had made some sweeping changes for no other reason than to please God. They were, in fact, sinning less than they ever had in their adult lives. Also, the woman claimed that God was making the babies sick and would see that they continued to suffer until their mother repented. That theory crumbled a day or so later when the kids got well.

I have no doubt that the lady was a highly respected member of her church. She may have taught a Sunday school class or headed the missions committee. I wouldn't be surprised if she was a tither and could quote ten times as many Bible verses as I can. I'm certainly not questioning her salvation or her intentions. But there's no doubt she was doing more harm than good on the afternoon that she paid our young mother a visit. Consider the results of her speculation, which I find are true of many Christians who speak above the level of their knowledge.

First, an already heavy burden was made even heavier. Paul made it clear that we are to bear one another's burdens, not add to them (see Galatians 6:2). But in the aftermath of the woman's visit, shoulders that were already sagging under the weight of worry and fatigue suddenly had a load of guilt to contend with. When we arrived at the young woman's house, she was sobbing uncontrollably.

Second, a passage of Scripture was horribly twisted. We're exhorted to correctly explain the word of truth (see 2 Timothy 2:15) and to minister to people with what the apostle Paul calls "good teaching" (2 Timothy 4:2). But the neighbor lady offered the opposite. The Hebrews 12 passage that she used as the basis for her comments offers no reason to believe that God would ever cruelly inflict suffering on innocent children as a way of punishing their parents. In fact, no passage in the Bible teaches such a thing!

Third, a terrible lie about God was perpetuated. The Bible teaches that God is love (see 1 John 4:16) and that the heart of the gospel is grace (see Ephesians 2:8). It says very clearly that He is unwilling for any to perish (see 2 Peter 3:15). Yet, Satan has always used people like the neighbor lady to promote the notion that God is an angry taskmaster who loves to punish people. And we can understand why Satan would do this. By diverting attention away from God's grace, he is diverting attention away from salvation, for the two are intimately and eternally intertwined. I can just imagine God groaning in frustration and Satan snickering when people like the neighbor lady yammer on and on about God's wrath and never think to mention His love, mercy, or grace.

It scares me to think what might have happened to that young mother if her neighbor had gotten a hold of her before she and her husband started going to church. Without a pastor or a friend to show her what the Bible really says, how would she have processed such cruel words? Perhaps she would have pegged the lady as a wacky religious fanatic and laughed the whole thing off. Or maybe she would have seethed with anger toward God, just as any mother would toward anybody she believed had hurt her children. Either way, it's hard to imagine her feeling favorable toward the Lord or His people . . . perhaps ever again.

Are you starting to understand why speaking above the level of your knowledge is such a serious blunder and why it needs to be taken seriously?

FIRST, DO NO HARM

Hippocrates was a Greek physician who was born around 470 BC. He is credited with writing the Hippocratic oath, which most physicians still quote in one form or another when they enter medical practice. Some people question whether the familiar phrase "First, do no harm" was ever a part of the oath, but even if it wasn't, the sentiment certainly was. A doctor's solemn duty has always been to use his knowledge and skills to make a patient better, or at least not to make him worse.

It seems to me this would be a good vow for all of us to take with regard to our speech. Everybody knows that lying, gossiping, and rumormongering are extremely harmful. But as I've just shown you, so is speaking above the level of your knowledge. I'm challenging you right now to get serious about this egregious blunder

—to adopt a "first, do no harm" mentality and stick to it through every conversation. In order to be successful, you will have to resist four temptations.

The Temptation to Analyze People

First, you will have to resist the temptation to analyze people. Many years before the advent of Women of Faith, I served a small church that had an active women's ministry. One day, the leader of that ministry told me she wanted to organize a "women's only" prayer chain. In case you're not familiar with the term, a prayer chain is simply a list of church members' names and phone numbers. If someone in the church has an urgent need, he or she calls the first name on the list, gives a brief description of the need, and requests prayer. Then that person calls the next number, and so on, until everyone on the list has been notified and is praying. It's a simple program that many churches employ, and the leader of our women's ministry wanted to organize one that only women would be allowed to be a part of.

However, I discouraged the idea. As pleasantly as possible, I explained that we already had a prayer chain that included both men and women. It was functioning beautifully, and I saw no reason to tamper with it. It seemed to me that adding a second prayer chain would create confusion. In addition, I pointed out that prayer is something everybody ought to be involved in, not just the ladies.

At the next meeting of the women's ministry, the leader reported my response and added an editorial comment. According to several witnesses, she said, "I think it's pretty obvious that Mark has a hang-up with women. I think we intimidate him." Whether she really thought that, I have no idea. Maybe she was just frustrated and couldn't resist tossing out a barb. Either way, she was speaking far above and beyond the level of her knowledge. There was not an ounce of truth in her comment.

But I must admit that I've done the same thing. Whenever somebody says or docs something that strikes me as odd, or that doesn't sit well, I'm always tempted to offer my less-than-expert analysis. Over the years, I've pegged people as lazy, jealous, self-centered, arrogant, and who knows what else when, honestly, I had no idea if they were or not. I was just reacting emotionally to something they said or did.

Of course, this sort of thing has been going on for a long time. You may recall that when young David offered to fight Goliath, his older brother, Eliab, was quick to analyze—or should I say *misanalyze*—his motives. He said, "What are you doing around here anyway? . . . What about those few sheep you're supposed to be taking care of? I know about your pride and dishonesty. You just want to see the battle!" (1 Samuel 17:28 NLT). Eliab, like so many of us, was speaking well above the level of his knowledge and ended up looking like a fool.

We would do well to remember that analyzing people (which is just another name for judging) is condemned in Scripture. Paul said, "Be careful not to jump to conclusions before the Lord returns as to whether or not someone is faithful. When the Lord comes, he will bring our deepest secrets to light and will reveal our private motives. And then God will give to everyone whatever praise is due" (1 Corinthians 4:5 NLT).

The next time you're tempted to blurt out an analysis of someone you dislike or disagree with, remember that only God is wise enough (and fair enough) to make judgments regarding another person's deepest secrets and private motives. Any attempt you or I might make in that direction would almost certainly require us to step beyond the limits of our knowledge, where the chances of our hurting others and embarrassing ourselves increase exponentially.

The Temptation to Explain Suffering

Second, if you want to do no harm in your conversations, you must resist the temptation to explain suffering. It doesn't matter if you're talking about AIDS, SARS, the 9/11 terrorist attacks, or three little preschoolers with the flu. For some reason, when we see suffering, we feel compelled to try to explain it. And, of course, because we're believers, we usually do it by attaching some spiritual significance to the pain. Like the Bible-toting neighbor I mentioned earlier, we generally assume that somebody's been misbehaving and that God's on the warpath.

And again, this is nothing new. In Luke 13, we learn that the Tower of Siloam fell and crushed eighteen men to death. Immediately, it was assumed that those men were the worst sinners in Jerusalem and that God was paying them back (see Luke 13:4).

The reason why it's pointless to try to explain suffering is because it isn't always the result of sin. Sometimes it's the result of faithfulness. And the purpose of it isn't always to punish. It can also be intended to strengthen. The apostle Paul would be a case in point. He suffered more than any ten men I know (see 2 Corinthians 11:23–27) and was even given a "thorn in the flesh," which caused him discomfort for years (see 2 Corinthians 12:7). But it wasn't because he was doing anything wrong. It was because he was doing almost everything right!

Or you could think about Job. The Bible says he was "blameless," a man of complete integrity. "He feared God and stayed away from evil" (Job 1:1 NLT). Yet, unimaginable suffering came pouring into his life.

What business do any of us have trying to explain suffering? Who among us has enough knowledge of the ways of God to always know what He's up to? Sure, there are some cases where suffering is clearly the consequence of sin. But we walk on thin ice when we try to put every bad thing that happens into some sort of spiritual context. What we should concentrate on instead is ministering to those hurting people and pointing them to "the source of every mercy and the God who comforts us" (2 Corinthians 1:3 NLT).

The Temptation to Spread Rumors

Third, if you want to do no harm in your conversations, you must resist the temptation to spread rumors. In one of my favorite episodes of *The Andy Griffith Show*, Barney has a cut on his finger. As a favor, Andy stops in at the drugstore to pick up some medicine. There he encounters Aunt Bee and two other ladies who ask if anyone is hurt. Andy casually explains that Barney hurt his finger cleaning his gun and leaves. The next thing you know, rumors are flying all over Mayberry about Barney Fife accidentally shooting himself. And in the final hilarious scene of the sequence, Barney actually takes a call at the courthouse from someone who is calling to report the death of Barney Fife!

But in real life, rumors are not funny.

You're probably familiar with the name J. K. Rowling. She's the author of the wildly popular Harry Potter novels. As her books were gaining popularity, a rumor started circulating that she was a witch and that her novels were an attempt to recruit young people to witchcraft. And this wasn't just a whispered rumor passing from one ear to another. It was circulated throughout the world via e-mail! Millions of people read this information and formed a very negative opinion of Ms. Rowling, even though it wasn't true.[2]

And who do you think took the most delight in forwarding that inaccurate e-mail?

Believers.

Christians couldn't click their Forward Mail icons fast enough. They thought they were doing a service to their brothers and sisters, when all they were really doing was spreading a lie.

Let me hasten to say that I believe a debate about the content of Ms. Rowling's novels is fair. Some believers feel that they do indeed glorify witchcraft, whether intentionally or not. But debating that issue is a far cry from unfairly and inaccurately branding someone a witch.

Proverbs 10:19 says, "Don't talk too much, for it fosters sin. Be sensible and turn off the flow!" (NLT). I like that imagery. The next time a juicy rumor comes your way, picture an open spigot with sin gushing forth. And then consider that your response will be a crank of that spigot's handle to either the left or the right. (Remember: lefty loosey; righty tighty.) If you can manage to keep your mouth shut, you will have given that puppy a hard crank to the right and done everybody a huge favor . . . especially the person the rumor was intended to hurt.

The Temptation to Believe Everything You Hear

Finally, if you want to do no harm in your conversations, you must resist the temptation to believe everything you hear. Back in 1999, a woman in Mobile, Alabama, claimed that she was approached in the parking lot of the bank where she worked by another woman selling perfume. The seller invited the bank employee to take a whiff of the fragrance and sprayed a mist of it toward her face. The next thing the woman knew, she was stretched out on the concrete, slowly emerging from a state of unconsciousness. Her purse was empty, and the eight hundred dollars she was carrying (which belonged to her employer) was gone. The woman claimed that she had been sprayed with ether, which caused her to pass out and enabled the con artist to make off with her valuables.

Even though no witnesses or investigators were ever able to corroborate the incident, and even though most people connected with the case believed the bank employee stole the money and concocted the story as a cover-up, it wasn't long before an alarming e-mail was flying around the country. I still remember the day it landed in my in-box. It warned that women walking alone through shopping center parking lots were being targeted by fake perfume saleswomen all around the country. As the father of a single adult female who often goes places alone, this was not good news. All sorts of scary scenarios started flashing through my mind.

But then I slammed on the brakes.

Before I forwarded the e-mail to my daughter, I decided to do some research. What I discovered was that a puff of ether from a perfume bottle would not be enough to render a person unconscious. In fact, a concoction that powerful would also be a threat to the person doing the spraying. The only way ether could be a threat to someone's consciousness would be if it were soaked into a handkerchief and clamped over the person's nose and mouth so that they had no choice but to breathe in the fumes.

I never forwarded that e-mail to my daughter. The story just seemed too fishy. And sure enough, it's now been granted "urban legend" status. The e-mail still makes the rounds every couple of years, but as of this writing, no incident of the sort it describes has been verified anywhere in the country.

Did you know the church has its own urban legends?

I'll never forget the guy who came to my office to tell me about his afterlife experience. He said he was on the operating table when his heart stopped. He saw a bright light (don't they all?), then Jesus with outstretched arms. While the doctors scrambled to get his heart restarted, Jesus spoke to him. It was the old I'm-not-through-with-you-so-I'm-sending-you-back message.

It was a nice story, but I never believed a word of it. Why? Because the guy was a lukewarm Christian at best. I saw him at church only a couple of times a month, he wasn't involved in any ministries and, by his own admission, didn't tithe. I'm sorry, but any man who says he's met the Lord face-to-face and actually heard Him speak better be on fire if he expects me to believe him. I don't see how anyone could really have that experience and then be apathetic about the things of God.

The Bible warns us not to believe every person who claims to have had a vision, heard a voice, or received some sort of miraculous intervention. Paul said, "Please don't be so easily shaken and troubled by those who say that the day of the Lord has already begun. Even if they claim to have had a vision, a revelation, or a letter supposedly from us, don't believe them. Don't be fooled by what they say" (2 Thessalonians 2:2–3 NLT). And Jude 1:8 warns that false teachers will use dreams and visions to try to establish their authority, then use that authority to lead people astray.

Am I saying we should reject everything that seems odd or

extraordinary? Absolutely not! We serve a miracle-working God who can accomplish far beyond anything we can ask or think (see Ephesians 3:20). But we mustn't be gullible. We must "test the spirits" (1 John 4:1 NKJV) and make sure a story (and the person telling it) has credibility before we start repeating it. And above all, we must never allow people's experiences, however thrilling they might be, to replace God's Word as the foundation of our preaching and teaching and belief. In the end, it's not what men have experienced, but what God has said that matters.

THE APOLLOS APPROACH

Before I close this chapter, I want to talk about what you should do if anyone ever accuses you of speaking above the level of your knowledge. You might have complete confidence in what you're saying. Indeed, the idea being challenged could be one you've believed and promoted for years in good faith. But when you least expect it, someone could walk up to you and tell you you're mistaken.

What would you do?

If you're like most people, your initial reaction would be to bristle and defend yourself, or perhaps to dismiss the person as a troublemaker. But I'd like to suggest a different approach.

The Apollos Approach.

In case you're not familiar with Apollos, his first appearance on the stage of Scripture is in Acts 18:

Meanwhile, a Jew named Apollos, an eloquent speaker who knew the Scriptures well, had just arrived in Ephesus from Alexandria in

Egypt. He had been taught the way of the Lord and talked to others with great enthusiasm and accuracy about Jesus. However, he knew only about John's baptism. (vv. 24–25 NLT)

Those two verses are of vital importance because they show that even a dedicated believer with the purest of hearts and best of intentions can spread misinformation. Apollos loved the Lord and wanted nothing more than to spread the gospel, but his message was incomplete. He knew about the baptism of repentance practiced by John (see Matthew 3:6), but he didn't know about the baptism of forgiveness that was instituted by Peter and the apostles on the day of Pentecost (see Acts 2:38). In other words, his theology was lagging behind the plan of God.

But one day a couple of believers who *were* up to speed heard him speak:

> When Priscilla and Aquila heard him preaching boldly in the synagogue, they took him aside and explained the way of God more accurately. (Acts 18:26 NLT)

I like that they took him aside. They didn't embarrass him in front of his listeners, but talked to him in private and explained how his message was lacking. What's conspicuously missing from the story is any indication that Apollos rejected their input. Nothing is said about an argument or any lingering friction. On the contrary, Apollos made the adjustment in his theology and was warmly embraced by the entire Christian community. Ultimately, he received their blessing as he went to Achaia and became a powerful force for the Lord:

When he arrived there, he proved to be of great benefit to those who, by God's grace, had believed. He refuted all the Jews with powerful arguments in public debate. Using the Scriptures, he explained to them, "The Messiah you are looking for is Jesus." (Acts: 27–28 NLT)

My point is this: Someday your very own Priscilla and Aquila might approach you and tell you you're speaking above the level of your knowledge. I hope they do it as gently as the original Priscilla and Aquila. But even if they don't, you'll be wise to take the Apollos approach. Don't blow them off. Listen to what they have to say. Carefully consider their thoughts in light of everything you know about the Scriptures. If you need to, dig deeper into the Word to verify either their ideas or yours. But don't dismiss them too quickly. God could be trying to bring you up to speed. Either way, you'll be wiser for having examined their ideas.

As I'm writing these words, the annual *Sports Illustrated* swimsuit edition has just hit newsstands and is attracting a lot of attention. This morning on one of the cable news programs, one of the *SI* models did the weather. When she was finished, some of her photos were flashed on the screen, causing the male hosts to stammer and stutter like silly schoolboys. I'm pretty sure when that young woman auditioned for the photo shoot, she wasn't asked to stick out her tongue. In fact, of the pictures that were flashed on the screen this morning, not one emphasized that particular part of her anatomy. Yet, I contend it is the tongue that is ultimately responsible for determining any person's beauty, male or female. Even a drop-dead gorgeous supermodel will eventually achieve hag status if her words are continually unpleasant. Don't you suppose this explains, at least in part, why some of the most beautiful men and women in the world can't seem to stay married?

Do you want to be thought of as a beautiful person?

Then don't gossip.

Don't judge.

Don't criticize.

Don't utter a single sentence unless you know exactly what you're talking about.

I can't promise that *Sports Illustrated* will come calling, but I can guarantee that the people you rub shoulders with will see you as a beautiful person in the way that really matters.

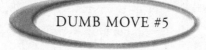

Hopping from Church to Church

We treat church with a consumer mentality—looking for the best product for the price of our Sunday morning. As a result, we're fickle and not invested for the long-term, like a lover with a wandering eye, always on the hunt for something better.

—JOSHUA HARRIS

Many Christians have a tendency to "hop" from church to church without ever settling down in one place and making a long-term commitment. I call them the "hopping fraternity," and I know they're not going to like this chapter. I've known a lot of church hoppers over the years, and they are always ready to defend their actions. In their minds, every hop is justified.

But I beg to differ.

I see church hopping as an enormous blunder that does more harm to the cause of Christ than many of us realize. That doesn't mean a person should never change churches. I pointed out in chapter 2 that there are times when it would be wrong *not* to look for another church home. But right now I intend to show you why, in the vast majority of cases, church hopping is counter-productive. So if you have a hopping history, or if you're a little dissatisfied with your church and you've been noticing what beautiful green grass the church down the street has, please don't make any decisions until you've finished this chapter.

TWO BREEDS OF CHURCH HOPPERS

I want to begin by pointing out that not all church hoppers are alike. There are two different kinds that I've run into over the years.

The Complainers

First, there are the complainers. A few years ago I received a phone call from a preacher buddy of mine who lived in the next county. I still recall the conversation as clearly as if it happened yesterday.

My Friend: Mark, I just wanted to let you know that you're probably going to have a visitor on Sunday morning.

Me: Oh really? Who?

My Friend: His name is _____ _____. He's been attending here for the last couple of years, but he's mad at us and says he's going to another church.

Me: Why on earth would he come over here? We're almost thirty miles from you.

My Friend: (Laughing) Because he's out of options in this area. He's attended and quit every church of our brotherhood in the entire county. Geographically, you're the next closest, so I figure you're next. I just thought I'd tip you off.

Me: You mean "warn" me, don't you?

My Friend: (Laughing again) Well, I guess you could say that.

Me: (Sighing) Oh, brother.

My Friend: (Sounding so cheerful it was annoying) Look on the bright side. He's never stayed in any church more than two years. So if you can just hang in there, he'll soon be moving on.

My friend was right. The man and his wife did show up the following Sunday morning. They came in smiling and shaking hands like the president and first lady during a tight political campaign. And when they introduced themselves to me, they really poured on the schmooze. He said, while vigorously pumping my hand, "We've heard so much about this church, we just decided to come over and see what all the excitement is about." I had to stifle the urge to step back and scream, "Liar, liar, pants on fire!"

Further, my friend was right about them not staying more than two years. In fact, I guess we were an especially poor excuse for a church in their minds because they only stuck with us for about fifteen months. I won't bore you with a list of their complaints. Suffice it to say, they pretty much found fault with everything we did and left thinking I was the devil.

But here's the funny part.

The day after they stormed out in a huff, I picked up the phone and called another preacher friend who lived about twelve miles farther on down the road. Our conversation went almost exactly like the one quoted above, only I was on the giving end this time.

I couldn't help smiling as I heard my friend sighing on the other end of the line. (I'm sure he thought the cheerful sound of my voice was thoroughly annoying.)

Well, guess what.

I was right!

The man and his wife did indeed show up at my buddy's church the very next Sunday. At that point, they were driving close to forty miles to church and passing by a half dozen fine congregations on the way. That was a few years ago. I figure by now they may be attending church in a neighboring state.

The complaining church hopper is never satisfied. He finds fault with everything the church does and foolishly believes the church down the highway will be exactly what he's looking for.

The Consumers

And then there are the consumers. This is the new breed of church hopper. With so many new churches springing up and offering such a rich diversity of worship styles, preaching styles, and programming, there can be a smorgasbord of fascinating possibilities in a single community. It's like having a McDonald's, a Burger King, and a Wendy's on the same street in your neighborhood. You may prefer the fries at McDonald's, the Whopper at Burger King, and a Wendy's Frosty for your sweet tooth. Consequently, you end up frequenting all three places, depending on your mood.

Likewise, Church A might have an awesome worship band, while Church B has a preacher you love to listen to. But then one of your buddies who attends Church C asks you to play on their softball team. Is this a problem? Of course not! You just do what any good consumer would do. You hop back and forth between the three churches.

In his book *Stop Dating the Church*, Joshua Harris tells about a friend of his who attended two churches every Sunday. He preferred the music at one church, so he stayed until the last song was winding down. Then he slipped out quietly and drove to another church that offered what he felt was better preaching. The arrangement was made even more satisfying by the fact that he always had time to stop and get an Egg McMuffin on the way.[1]

I know the same kind of thing happens at Poinciana Christian Church. Recently, two unmarried women who are apparently unable to whisper happened to be sitting behind my wife. When I announced that I was launching a new sermon series on the subject of marriage, Marilyn overheard one of them say, "Oh, brother! Let's just go to the Baptist Church until he gets done with this series." And they did.

WHO INVENTED CHURCH HOPPING?

Any high school freshman knows that Alexander Graham Bell invented the telephone.

Thomas Edison invented the incandescent bulb.

Robert Fulton invented the steamboat.

Walt Disney invented Mickey Mouse.

And Al Gore invented the Internet.

But who invented church hopping? Who came up with this notion that you should never settle down and commit to a church until you find one that's perfect in every way?

Satan did, that's who.

Oh, I know the members of the church-hopping fraternity will probably be hopping mad when they read this. I will probably get a stack of angry e-mails as high as my head. I know from having spoken to many of them that church hoppers are always eager to defend their actions. (And some of them have their spiels quite polished, I might add.) But I still think Satan is behind this phenomenon, and I don't make that statement lightly. For more than thirty years I've been watching believers hop in and out of the churches I've served, and there are six conclusions I've drawn.

CONCLUSION #1: CHURCH HOPPERS TEND TO BE VERY CRITICAL. We should know by now that there's no such thing as a perfect church. You'll notice areas that need improvement in even the most vibrant and successful churches if you attend long enough. What I've noticed about church hoppers is that they walk through the door like Sherlock Holmes peering through a magnifying glass, determined to find the flaws. Why? Because flaws are their license to keep hopping.

Test me on this.

The next time you encounter a church hopper, ask him why he left his last church. I guarantee he will not say, "It's my problem. The church was awesome, but I just have trouble making a commitment." Instead, he'll immediately start telling you about some great weakness the church had that he just couldn't live with. He'll explain how that flaw was a hindrance to his walk with the Lord, and he'll talk about how he just needed to find something better.

Such an attitude reminds me of a story I once heard about a castle with seven guest bedrooms. Six of the bedrooms looked out over beautiful gardens and lush, rolling meadows, while the seventh looked out over the place where the castle's garbage was collected. One time, seven foreign dignitaries arrived for a visit and each was assigned one of the bedrooms. When they left, six of the dignitaries went home and told family and friends what a beautiful place they had just visited, while the seventh reported that it was a dump.

Churches, like castles, produce a certain amount of garbage simply because people are imperfect. That means if you look through enough windows, you're eventually going to find an unattractive view. In my experience, a chronic church hopper won't quit looking until he finds the window that overlooks the dump. He needs to find that garbage pile so he can use it as Exhibit A when he gets the itch to move on.

CONCLUSION #2: CHURCH HOPPERS TEND TO HAVE A "ME FIRST" ATTITUDE. When somebody hops into our church from a nearby congregation, I'm always leery. There have been some cases where the person had what I felt were honorable and legitimate reasons for making the change, but I'd have to say that at least 75 percent of the time I have detected the faint smell of something foul in the air. In fact, there is one comment I have heard more than any other, and when I hear it I know I might as well clamp a clothespin on my nose because what follows is really going to stink.

"I left that church because I just wasn't being fed."

If, somewhere in this world, there is a school for church hoppers, that statement must be what students are required to memorize on the first day of class, because 99 percent of the church hoppers I've ever known have used it. And why not? It has a nice spiritual ring to it and makes the poor soul sound like he's only concerned about growing in the Lord. Also, if the individual happened to be in conflict with the pastor or church leaders of his former church (which is not unusual), it serves as a subtle put-down . . . an insult that doesn't really sound like an insult.

But let's think about this comment.

When a church hopper says he wasn't being fed, isn't he implying that he was starving spiritually? But why would any supposedly mature Christian ever starve? With all the new Bible translations, software packages, study aids, teaching conferences, and wonderful Christian books that are available nowadays, how is it possible that a conscientious Christian could be malnourished?

Unless he's sitting around waiting to be *spoon*-fed.

My advice for any starving Christian is to pick up your fork and eat! If the pastor of your church isn't the most dynamic speaker in the world, so what? One of my best friends is married to a woman who isn't the greatest cook in the world, but he's still carrying an extra ten pounds around his middle! He may have to work a little harder for his calories than some guy who lives with a gourmet chef, but in our land of plenty, if he starves it's his own fault.

The bottom line: Chronic church hoppers love to be catered to, doted on, and spoon-fed. And when they aren't, they're gone.

CONCLUSION #3: CHURCH HOPPERS ALMOST NEVER GET INVOLVED. The command to serve God is one of the most basic in the Bible. First Corinthians 12:7 says, "A spiritual gift is given to each of us as a means of helping the entire church" (NLT).

But let's face it. You can't serve faithfully if you don't attend faithfully. You can't be put on a ministry schedule if you're going to show up only when the mood strikes you. You can't be counted on by one church if you're going to spend half your time at another church. If you've ever been a ministry coordinator and have tried to work with part-timers who are "hit and miss" in their attendance, you know what a nightmare it is.

Some church hoppers I've known have tried to wiggle off the hook on this point by suggesting that they don't need to serve *inside* the church to be faithful to the Lord. They say it's perfectly acceptable for them to serve *outside* the framework of the church's ministry. For example, one church hopper I know, who isn't involved in any church-related ministry, points to his work as a Little League coach. He says he witnesses to the kids and, therefore, is fulfilling his obligation to serve God. While I applaud his willingness to work with kids and his desire to influence them for Christ, I have a hard time reconciling his position with Scripture.

The Bible says we are to "serve *each other*" (1 Peter 5:5 NLT, emphasis added).

It says we are to "teach and counsel *each other*" (Colossians 3:16 NLT, emphasis added).

It says we are to "do good to *each other*" (1 Thessalonians 5:15 NLT, emphasis added).

It says we are to "encourage and warn *each other*" (Hebrews 10:25 NLT, emphasis added).

The words *each other* make it obvious that these acts of service and ministry are supposed to be happening *within* the church. And we see it almost from day one. As early as Acts 6, there were already food distribution programs being organized to make sure every member's needs were being met!

So let's be honest. While it's fine to coach a Little League team and witness to your players, that doesn't exempt a person from serving within the framework of the church's ministry. God has always intended for service and ministry to happen inside the body of Christ. But that can't happen without people who settle in and become steadfastly committed and involved.

CONCLUSION #4: CHURCH HOPPERS ALMOST NEVER MAKE A SERIOUS FINANCIAL INVESTMENT IN THE CHURCH.

Check the giving records of any congregation, and you'll see that the church hoppers in the crowd carry almost none of the financial load.

A few years ago, I happened to be the last one leaving our building after Sunday morning services. I was just getting into my car when a late-model Cadillac pulled up beside me. Inside was a couple who had hopped into our church from another congregation in the area. I had checked with their former pastor and learned that they never stayed in one place very long. However, they seemed like nice people, and I was hoping that maybe they would settle in with us and get involved.

As the car rolled to a stop, the passenger-side window slid down and the lady said, "Pastor Mark, we left our checkbook at home this morning, so we ran right home after the service and wrote out our check for the offering. I'm glad you were still here to take it." She held her envelope out to me. I took it and thanked them for being so thoughtful. But as they drove away, I looked at the envelope and on the line where the amount is to be designated, she had written, "$5.00." Five dollars from two people who lived in a two-hundred-thousand-dollar home and drove a thirty-five-thousand-dollar car. Would it surprise you if I told you they stayed with us less than a year?

In Matthew 6:21, Jesus tied our hearts and wallets up in a nice, neat little bundle. He said, "Wherever your treasure is, there your heart and thoughts will also be" (NLT). A person's heart and his treasure are always going to be found in the same place. So if a church hopper's heart isn't in the local church (and it never is), his or her money won't be either.

CONCLUSION #5: CHURCH HOPPERS MAKE IT A POINT TO REMAIN EMOTIONALLY DETACHED. They know if they start making close friends, it will be hard for them to move on when the itch strikes. So you generally won't find them attending a Sunday school class, joining a small group, or participating in fellowship events.

This is a very dangerous way to live the Christian life.

If there's one doctrine the Bible hammers home relentlessly, it's the idea that we need one another. Of course, we need God. But the Bible writers made it clear that we also need to be heavily invested in relationships with other believers if we hope to survive in this mean old world and reach our potential. Ecclesiastes 4:12 says, "A person standing alone can be attacked and defeated, but two can stand back-to-back and conquer. Three are even better, for a triple-braided cord is not easily broken" (NLT). And Proverbs 27:17 says, "As iron sharpens iron, a friend sharpens a friend" (NLT).

It's also worth noting that the early church made fellowship a top priority. Acts 2:42 says, "They joined with the other believers and devoted themselves to the apostles' teaching and fellowship, sharing in the Lord's Supper and in prayer" (NLT). Later, Paul commended the Thessalonians for their emphasis on relationship building. He said, "Dear brothers and sisters, we always thank God for you, as is right, for we are thankful that your faith is flourishing and *you are all growing in love for each other*" (2 Thessalonians 1:3 NLT, emphasis added).

At the same time, if there's one thing Satan hates, it's a tightly woven body of believers. When God's people lock arms and commit to watching out for one another, his opportunities are greatly reduced. So it stands to reason that he would slink away in search of someone who has little, if any, support system. First Peter 5:8 says, "He prowls around like a roaring lion, looking for some victim to devour" (NLT).

CONCLUSION #6: CHURCH HOPPERS ENJOY LIVING FREE FROM ACCOUNTABILITY. One of the most powerful lessons God taught His infant church had to do with accountability. In Acts 5, we're told that a couple named Ananias and Sapphira sold a piece of property and told everyone they were donating the entire sale price to the church, when in fact they were keeping some of the money for themselves. Peter called Ananias in and confronted him on the matter, only to watch him drop dead in his tracks. Three hours later, Sapphira was called in and given an opportunity to confess her sin and set the record straight. When she didn't, she, too, keeled over.

The telling verse, however, is Acts 5:11: "Great fear gripped the entire church and all others who heard what had happened" (NLT). I picture God in heaven, nodding His approval at the fear He saw in His people, not because He is a bully and enjoys terrorizing His children, but because He wanted to send them a clear and unmistakable message: "In My church there are certain standards of behavior, and you will be held accountable for your actions."

To further emphasize the importance of accountability, and to set up a system where it could function in a consistent way, God established the eldership. Acts 14:23 says, "Paul and Barnabas . . . appointed elders in every church and prayed for them with fast-ing, turning them over to the care of the Lord, in whom they had come to trust" (NLT). What were the elders to do? Among other things, they were to shepherd God's flock (see Acts 20:28).

There are several terms that describe the shepherding ministry of the elders. One I've often used is "referee." Good elders watch for and "blow the whistle" on conduct that would be harmful to the body. But, of course, they have jurisdiction over only the specific flock they're a part of. That means a church hopper, because he hasn't officially identified himself with any one church, is virtually exempt from any oversight. He can do whatever he wants and knows he won't have to answer to a guy with a whistle and a striped shirt.

I'm not saying that church hoppers are chronic misbehavers who always need to have the whistle blown on them. My point is that God has set things up so that His people can be held accountable for their actions, but believers who want to "beat the system" can do so simply by refusing to commit to any one church.

So let's review before we move on. Church hoppers . . .

- □ tend to be very critical,
- □ tend to have a "me first" attitude,
- □ almost never get involved,
- □ almost never make a serious financial investment in the church,
- □ make it a point to remain emotionally detached,
- □ and enjoy living free from accountability.

These are the reasons why I believe the concept of church hopping has the devil's fingerprints all over it. There's absolutely nothing about it that benefits the body of Christ, nor is it healthy for the believer. To seal my case, just imagine what the body of Christ would be like if every believer were a church hopper. Obviously, there would be no such thing as healthy, established congregations with functioning ministries and outreach programs because those things are always built by people who settle in and commit for the long haul.

THE BLESSINGS OF A
LONG-TERM COMMITMENT

If there's one group of people who could almost justify church hopping, it would be those who've made ministry their vocation. For example, as a pastor, I get calls from other churches asking if I might be willing to leave my current church and be their preacher. Sometimes those calls come when I am frustrated or disappointed with the way things are going at Poinciana Christian. Or sometimes they come when I'm dealing with someone who seems intent on driving me out of my mind. At such times, it's always tempting to say, "Yes, I can come and be your preacher. Would it be okay if I arrived first thing in the morning?"

Rest assured, all ministry professionals occasionally entertain thoughts of hopping right out the door, and a good many act on those thoughts with alarming regularity. Statistics vary, but it's generally accepted that the average length of ministry for pastors is somewhere between two and four years. If church hopping were an Olympic sport, we pastors would hold more than our share of gold, silver, and bronze.

During the seventeen-plus years that I've been the pastor of PCC, I suppose I've been tempted to leave at least once a year, and sometimes more. Some of those temptations were so tantalizing I could hardly stand it. But God gave me the wisdom to stay put every time, and for that I'm truly thankful. Why? Because now I can see so clearly that there are tremendous blessings to be found in a long-term commitment to one church. It doesn't matter if you're the senior pastor or a member of the rank and file, wonderful things will start happening when years of faithful service begin to pile up.

FIRST, SERVING FAITHFULLY IN ONE CHURCH OVER THE LONG HAUL WILL GIVE YOU A SENSE OF BELONGING. If you want to know how important this is, just ask a child of divorce who's constantly being shuffled back and forth between two households. Or ask a college freshman who's living away from home for the first time and suddenly finds himself rooming with someone who doesn't share his moral convictions. Or ask a single person whose close friends are all married. Or ask a fifty-five-year-old who's just gotten laid off and is trying to find a job.

You get the picture.

Lots of people live every day with the feeling of not fitting in, not having a place, or not being accepted. Comedian George Gobel was describing that feeling when he quipped to Johnny Carson, "Do you ever feel like the world is a tuxedo and you're a pair of brown shoes?"

What I love is that the true body of Christ welcomes everybody. Paul said it in 1 Corinthians 12:13: "Some of us are Jews, some are Gentiles, some are slaves, and some are free. But we have all been baptized into Christ's body by one Spirit, and we have all received the same Spirit" (NLT). In other words, to use George Gobel's imagery, it doesn't matter if you're a spiffy pair of patent leathers or an old, worn-out pair of brown penny loafers, there is a place for you in the body of Christ. All you have to do is settle down in a healthy church and make a serious commitment. It won't be long until you'll start feeling right at home. In fact, you might even discover, as so many people have, that you feel more at home at church than you do at home!

SECOND, SERVING FAITHFULLY IN ONE CHURCH OVER THE LONG HAUL WILL GIVE YOU A SENSE OF ACCOMPLISHMENT. I like the story about the woman who banded together with eleven of her friends to form a weight-loss club. After one of their meetings, she came charging into the house full of excitement. She said to her husband, "We're really doing great. Between us we've lost 148 pounds!" Her husband said, "How many of those 148 pounds have you lost?" "Well . . . none," she answered, "but all together we've lost 148!"

Most of the church hoppers I've known have been exactly like that woman. They're ready at the drop of a hat to tell you about the successes of the church they happen to be attending at the moment, but they fail to mention the fact that they've contributed almost nothing. They remind me of the little mouse that was riding on the back of a huge elephant. As they were crossing a bridge, the spindly planks began to creak and moan. Suddenly, the bridge collapsed, dropping them to the ground with a resounding thud. As the dust began to clear, the tiny mouse looked up at the gigantic elephant and said, "I guess we were just too heavy."

A faithful, committed servant, on the other hand, doesn't have to pretend or imagine that he's making a contribution. He can *know* it because he can *see* it.

For example, in our church there is a young man named Rashad who plays Division I college football. His body looks like it's chiseled out of granite. (The Bible says we're going to get new bodies in heaven, and I've already put in my order for one just like his.) More important, he's an awesome young man. He's personable, polite, and respectful.

My wife talks about this young man often. When he comes home from college, she always mentions him and talks about how great he turned out. The reason she's so interested in him is because she was his Sunday school teacher for years when he was a little boy. She would never claim to have been the primary influence in his life. Indeed, the young man has an incredible mother. But Marilyn knows she had a small part in shaping him. There were many hours when he sat at her feet and listened to her talk about Jesus. She answered his childlike questions and guided his little hands in service projects. Seeing him today brings those memories back and fills her with joy. It's an experience you just can't have if you're constantly hopping from church to church.

THIRD, SERVING FAITHFULLY IN ONE CHURCH OVER THE LONG HAUL WILL LEAD YOU TO SOME WONDERFUL DISCOVERIES ABOUT YOURSELF. I once read a story about a man in the Old West who was appalled at the hand-lettered signs many of his town's merchants had put up in their store windows. Some of the signs had been scrawled on pieces of scrap metal and lumber with all the skill of a five-year-old. One day he was complaining to his wife about how ugly they looked and she said, "If you don't like them, why don't you do something about it? Get some paint and do them right. I'm sure the merchants would appreciate it."

Her husband said, "But I can't paint signs!"

"How do you know? You've never tried," his wife countered.

After thinking it over and deciding that he simply couldn't tolerate those signs any longer, the man decided to give sign painting a try. So he bought some paint and brushes and went to work in the privacy of his barn. Within a few days, he had replaced every ugly sign in town with one that had been carefully lettered.

But that's not the end of the story.

The merchants and townspeople were so pleased with his work that they encouraged him to open his own sign-painting business. He did, and became wealthier than he'd ever been in his life.

It's not unusual for things like that to happen to people who are faithfully serving in churches. I've known countless people who discovered hidden talents simply because there was a job that needed doing and no one else to do it.

One day our education director informed me that she had recruited two grandfathers to teach a first-grade-level class. Perhaps *recruited* isn't the right word. *Begged* would probably be more accurate. Honestly, I thought the choice had disaster written all over it. They were good guys, but neither of them had ever taught before, and I couldn't get the old dogs/new tricks adage out of my mind. Plus, I couldn't imagine them having the energy to keep up with a roomful of first graders. But she, having a lot more faith than I (and perhaps no other options), trained them and turned them loose.

To say they were successful would be an understatement. The kids loved them! I still remember those old guys walking the hallways of our education department with a conga line of little kids trailing along after them, laughing and squealing. And I remember the looks of absolute joy on those two old faces. I know they never dreamed they possessed such a gift!

FOURTH, SERVING FAITHFULLY IN ONE CHURCH OVER THE LONG HAUL WILL FILL YOUR LIFE WITH MEANINGFUL RELA-TIONSHIPS. In his book *The Purpose Driven Church*, Rick Warren tells about a survey one of his friends took in the church he served. The first question he asked his people was, "Why did you join this church?" Ninety-three percent of the members said, "I joined because of the pastor." The second question he asked was, "If the pastor leaves, will you leave?" It would be natural to assume that a good percentage of people said yes, considering the way they answered the first question. But that's not what happened. Ninety-three percent said they would *not* leave if the pastor left. When asked why, they said, "Because I have friends here!"[2]

Rick points out that such a shift in allegiance from the pastor to the people is perfectly normal and healthy. When you worship, work, laugh, cry, pray, and go to battle with people, incredibly strong bonds begin to develop.

Several years ago, a family in our church decided to escape the metro Orlando rat race by building a home on five acres in the country. Unfortunately for us, that five-acre plot was in the next county. When I first learned of their decision I was sad because they were good friends and were deeply involved in ministry. They were the kind of people every church hates to lose. I resigned myself to the fact that they would start attending a church closer to their new home.

However, they didn't.

Though their new house was fifty-two miles from our church

building, they continued to attend and serve as faithfully as ever for several years. Though it meant a 104-mile round-trip, they never missed a beat in their attendance or involvement, and the reason why can be summed up in one word: *relationships.* What they shared with certain people in our congregation was so meaningful and important to them, they were willing to sacrifice time and gas money to keep it alive.

Now, let me hasten to add that I would never ask or even recommend that a person drive so far to church if there's a good, Bible-believing congregation closer. However, the experience of the family I've just told you about illustrates how precious relationships that have been built over the long haul in a godly environment can become. No wonder Jesus said that our love for one another would be one of the distinguishing marks of our discipleship (see John 13:35).

FINALLY, SERVING FAITHFULLY IN ONE CHURCH OVER THE LONG HAUL WILL MAKE YOU A POWERFUL WITNESS FOR THE LORD. Some people think that in order to be a powerful witness you have to have either a heartrending testimony or a high-profile position, not to mention the gift of eloquence. But that's not true.

Let me tell you about Paul.

I was fresh out of Bible college and serving my first full-time church in a small town in southern Missouri. Paul, one of our members, was a tiny man, maybe five feet or so tall, and slightly retarded. I never really knew how old he was. I'm guessing he was in his fifties. He lived with his mother and swept the floor at a local grocery store. Almost every time I stopped in, he was in his apron, smiling and working that push broom as if he were expecting a visit from the president of the United States. Every conversation I ever had with Paul eventually got around to the subject of food. He was as skinny as a rail, but he loved food. Or maybe he just loved to talk about it.

To be honest, Paul could never have served on the church board or taught a class or chaired a committee. But there was one thing Paul did better than anybody else. When I concluded my ministry with that church in 1982, he hadn't missed a Sunday service in thirty-six years. That's perfect attendance going all the way back to 1946! A mind-boggling 1,872 straight Sundays that he showed up to worship the God he loved in his own simple way.

Don't think for a minute that Paul didn't have the absolute respect and admiration of everybody in that congregation. Sure, we knew his limitations. But we also knew he set the standard for faithfulness. In fact, I can't begin to count the number of times I've thought about him over the years and drawn inspiration from his example.

Occasionally, I meet a believer who seems exceptionally gifted and intelligent, but who's never settled down in one place long enough to get to know people, to earn their trust, and to make an impact. Usually, I find myself wondering what that person could accomplish if his talents and brainpower were coupled with Paul's brand of faithfulness.

To conclude this chapter, I'm going to make a statement that is going to sound pretty radical. But before you dismiss it (and me, as some kind of lunatic), I urge you to think it through. Here goes: *I believe God is disappointed in all chronic church hoppers.* I say that because there are so many critical New Testament commands a church-hopping believer simply cannot fulfill. For example, we're told to:

- Be devoted to one another (see Romans 12:10).
- Serve one another (see Galatians 5:13).
- Bind ourselves together (see Ephesians 4:3).
- Teach and counsel each other (see Colossians 3:16).
- Build each other up (see 1 Thessalonians 5:11).
- Live peaceably with each other (see 1 Thessalonians 5:13).
- Encourage and warn each other (see Hebrews 10:25).
- Confess our sins to each other and pray for each other (see James 5:16).
- Live in harmony with one another (see 1 Peter 3:8).

Any church hopper who says he can fulfill those commands in any meaningful way is living in a fantasy world. Look at the list again. Those are all activities that require a significant level of intimacy and trust, such as confessing sins to one another. Seriously now, do you really want to confess your sins to someone you see only occasionally and whom you barely know?

I didn't think so.

There's no doubt that God intends for all of His children to be committed to and intimately involved with a local church. Sometimes the circumstances of our lives require that we pull up stakes and move on. In our generation, that's common. But even when that happens, we should be on the lookout for another congregation to commit to.

It's what God wants.

It's what we need.

And it's what the world will notice.

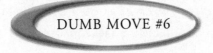

DUMB MOVE #6

Fighting Among
Ourselves

*Every gun that is made, every warship launched, every rocket
fired signifies in the final sense, a theft from those who hunger
and are not fed, those who are cold and not clothed.*

—DWIGHT D. EISENHOWER

They are the "Black Sheep," aka Second Platoon, A Company,
Second Battalion, Seventy-fifth Ranger Regiment. The talking
heads on the evening news refer to them as "Special Ops." We
know them simply as the good guys who do the dirty work in the
world's most dangerous places.

In April 2004, they were creeping through the desolate moun-
tains of eastern Afghanistan, trying to kill or capture al Qaeda and
Taliban fugitives that were believed to be hiding in the area. It's
arguably the most dangerous work a human being can do, but they
weren't complaining. For the Black Sheep, such work is a passion.

A calling of sorts. Heaven knows, you don't just wake up one morning and find that you're an Army Ranger.

At dusk one afternoon, the Black Sheep succeeded in flushing out some bad guys. With visibility diminishing rapidly, they knew they would have to engage the enemy immediately or risk losing them. Quickly, the Rangers fanned out, took up positions, and prepared to strike another blow for freedom.

That's when everything went horribly wrong.

A few of the Rangers ran to a position that was too far forward. Maneuvering for a more advantageous angle, they put themselves into the line of their comrades' fire without realizing it. Within that group was a bearded Afghan militia volunteer who was carrying an AK-47. At one point, he stood up and raised his weapon, silhouetting himself against the twilight sky.

When he did, he looked just like a Taliban fighter.

Suddenly, the unfortunate Rangers were under heavy fire from their own comrades. Gunners farther back poured an unrelenting barrage of rounds into their position. The Afghan volunteer never had a chance. He was riddled with bullets and died instantly. The reason we know about this incident is because someone else was killed, too. Someone Americans knew very well: Pat Tillman, the former NFL player who turned down a $3.6 million contract with the Arizona Cardinals to go fight for his country. Eyewitnesses said that a badly wounded Tillman lay on the ground screaming with his dying breath, "Cease fire! Friendlies!"[1]

When Tillman's death was first reported, no mention was made of fratricide. Army officials quickly awarded him a posthumous Silver Star and released a detailed account of his heroism. It was about a month later that they issued a brief statement indicating he was "probably" killed by friendly fire.

Friendly.

Fire.

Two harmless words until you put them side by side. Then they become unspeakably ugly. Horrifying enough when you're talking about war, but even more frightening when you're talking about church. I doubt that anything causes God more anguish and Satan more delight than Christians attacking one another.

Over the years, millions of people have suffered deep, sometimes spiritually fatal wounds within the body of Christ. You wouldn't think this would be the case. You'd like to believe the church would be a safe haven, a place where a person wouldn't have to worry about getting hurt. But almost from the beginning of time, believers have attacked one another. The first murder was triggered by jealousy and resentment over an act of worship (see Genesis 4:3–8), and God's people have been fussing and feuding ever since. In fact, a surprising amount of Scripture was written to settle conflicts between believers who were clawing at one another's throats.

And all this fighting has taken a toll.

One time I visited a family that had just adopted a dog. He was a cute little guy, but he was deathly afraid of people. When I tried to pet him, he cowered and backed away, trembling. It was obvious that he'd been abused.

As a pastor, I frequently meet people who are just like that little dog. They want nothing more than to be part of a loving church family, but nothing in their experience tells them such a thing exists. Oh, sure, they've read about love in the Bible and heard other people talking about their wonderful church experiences, but all *they've* ever known is conflict and division. In the various churches they've attended, they've been ignored, criticized, belittled, gossiped about, and harangued from the pulpit. When I meet them coming through the doors of our church, they may still be carrying the faint hope that this time things will be different, but you can tell they're gun-shy. They're very skeptical. Very slow to open up. Very hesitant to start investing themselves. And who can blame them?

THE FAR-REACHING FALLOUT
OF A FAMILY FEUD

The other day I was channel surfing and ran across an old rerun of *The Family Feud*. There was Richard Dawson in his plaid polyester suit, kissing every woman in sight and cracking lame jokes that should have gotten his scriptwriter fired. I was never a fan of the show, but I must admit that for a few minutes I had fun trying to guess what the audience surveys would reveal.

But in real life, family feuds are never fun . . . especially church family feuds. I can think of at least seven terrible things that always happen when a feud breaks out in the church.

FIRST, THE CHURCH'S LEADERS ARE DISTRACTED. Ask any church leader, and he will tell you that nothing eats up his time and saps his strength like trying to resolve conflicts between members. Time and energy that could be spent planning for the future, organizing new ministries, or seeing to it that the flock is well cared for, are instead spent chasing down rumors, smoothing ruffled feathers, and negotiating cease-fires.

I kept a record of the amount of time my elders and I spent helping two families in our church work through a dispute. We met with the parties involved to discuss their issues on four separate occasions. The total time of those meetings was 205 minutes. Times 5 (for the number of men involved) would make 1,025 minutes. Divided by 60 would make just over 17 man-hours invested. And that doesn't include the phone calls that were made and e-mails that were sent between meetings. Nor does it take into account the emotional stress of the whole affair.

And that was just one dispute! Imagine how much time and energy would be drained out of the leaders if there were several brewing at the same time!

SECOND, WHEN A FEUD BREAKS OUT IN THE CHURCH, THE NONCOMBATANTS ARE DISCOURAGED. One time Marilyn bought us tickets to a Tampa Bay Buccaneers football game for my birthday. I looked forward to going to the game for weeks, but when it was all over, I decided I'd probably never go back.

Why?

Because we ended up being surrounded by people who were probably born obnoxious, but became more obnoxious with every beer they drank. Before the game was over, four fights had broken out, several people had been hauled to jail (no, Marilyn wasn't among them), and armed police officers were permanently stationed in our section. I'm not exaggerating when I say that there were moments when we feared for our safety.

That evening as we drove home, I said all the same things an innocent bystander says who's caught in the middle of a strife-torn church.

"It's not supposed to be like this."

"Why can't people just get along?"

"It's all so petty and stupid."

"I don't know if I ever want to go back."

You see, you don't have to be involved in a fight for it to affect you. If you're just nearby, it will suck every ounce of enjoyment right out of whatever experience you happen to be having. At a football game, at work, or at church—it doesn't matter. After a while, you start telling yourself you must be nuts for putting up with it.

THIRD, WHEN A FEUD BREAKS OUT IN CHURCH, THE LORD'S WORK IS DISRUPTED. No, I don't mean that the Sunday services will be canceled or that the worship team will suddenly lay down their instruments and storm off in a huff. All the activities of the church will no doubt go on and, to the uninformed observer, look pretty normal. But those involved in the fracas will be so pre-occupied with trying to score points for their side that they won't be thinking about the real work the Lord has called them to do. They will see every conversation as an opportunity to vent, criticize, or lobby for their point of view, instead of an opportunity to talk about Jesus.

Many years ago, a hairdresser in the church I was serving became irate over a decision made by our leadership. It was an outstanding decision, but it cramped her style a little and she didn't like it one bit. It just so happened that several of our members went to her to get their hair done. One by one, her customers reported to me that she was openly blasting the elders and me in her shop. Every time a member came in that she thought might be sympathetic, she took the opportunity to spew venom. And she did it without regard for the other people sitting in the shop who could hear every word. Imagine all the good she could have done through those same conversations if she'd had a positive attitude.

It's safe to say that no Christian can advance the cause of Christ while punching the bride of Christ.

FOURTH, WHEN A FEUD BREAKS OUT IN CHURCH, THE COMMUNITY'S SEEKERS ARE DISENCHANTED. Imagine a woman with a heavy load of problems walking into that hair salon I just mentioned. Let's say she isn't religious, but is so desperate that she's been mulling over the idea of going to church. She doesn't know one from another, but she happens to drive by one on her way to work every day, and every time she does the urge gets a little stronger. She's almost made up her mind to throw caution to the wind and just do it . . . when she hears her hairdresser launch into an angry rant. She keeps her nose buried in a magazine, but she isn't reading. She's listening. And with every word she hears, the urge to go to church grows a little weaker.

If there's one thing I've learned, it's that seekers are everywhere. Sometimes they give off signals and make themselves known, but most of the time they don't. Either way, they're always around—at the beauty shop, the Little League game, the PTA meeting, or the car dealership. And they're always watching and listening. I shudder to think how many souls have been driven away from the Lord by thoughtless words spoken by quarrelsome Christians.

FIFTH, WHEN A FEUD BREAKS OUT IN CHURCH, LONG-HELD BELIEFS ARE DISREGARDED. One of my favorite novels is Robert

Louis Stevenson's *Dr. Jekyll and Mr. Hyde*. It's a creepy story about a gentleman physician who drinks a mysterious potion and transforms himself into a hideous monster. I've often recalled that book when I've watched believers who were otherwise kind and gentle suddenly become mean and ruthless in the middle of a church fight.

It never fails.

People who've always believed in forgiveness will suddenly be holding grudges. People who've always believed gossip is a sin will suddenly be blabbing all over town. People who've always believed friendship is one of life's most precious treasures will suddenly be snubbing their neighbors. And people who've always believed in telling the straight truth will suddenly be twisting it into the shape of a pretzel.

There's an old saying that all is fair in love and war. I don't know about the love part, but I've seen enough church wars to know that the rules of common decency are generally thrown right out the window like yesterday's garbage.

SIXTH, WHEN A FEUD BREAKS OUT IN CHURCH, THE CONGREGATION'S TESTIMONY IS DISCREDITED. It would be nice if only the people involved in the ruckus were stained by it, but that's not how it works. Instead, if church conflict persists, the entire body is branded.

Several years ago, I was contacted by a church that was interested in hiring me. I was curious about the offer, so I talked to some people who lived in that area and were familiar with the church. To my surprise, I got the same response again and again. They said it was a troubled church and that I'd be smart to steer clear of it. "That church chews preachers up and spits them out," one person said. Then I spoke to a man who had actually served there and got the inside scoop. He said there were only three or four troublemakers in the entire church, but it seemed there were more because they were so relentless. "Someday, when those few people are dead, it's going to be a nice place to serve," he said. "But until then, look out!"

And that's my point.

There were hundreds of people in that church who'd never done anything to deserve a bad reputation. But they had one just the same, thanks to a small handful of people who just couldn't seem to play nice.

FINALLY, WHEN A FEUD BREAKS OUT IN CHURCH, THE LORD IS DISHONORED. Not long ago I preached the strangest funeral of my thirty-plus years in the ministry. As I stood in the pulpit and looked out over the audience, I saw a family divided. The deceased man's children and their families were split into two groups. One group sat near the front of the auditorium and the other sat near the back. They were separated by at least eight empty rows, and neither group acknowledged the other's existence. Even though they were all brothers and sisters, cousins, aunts and uncles, at no time did they mingle or speak. When the service was over, they all got up and marched straight out the door.

Because I'd never met them (and because none of them spoke to me), I never got a clue as to what their problem was. But it was obvious a full-scale feud was in progress. When all was said and done, all I could think about was their dead father and how ashamed he would have been of their behavior. He'd been a nice man, and I know he taught them better than that.

Just as those sons and daughters blatantly dishonored their father, so we dishonor our Lord when we fight among ourselves. By pursuing our selfish agendas and ignoring His commands regarding love, acceptance, and forgiveness, we are essentially telling Him and the rest of the world that His will is of little importance to us.

As I was writing this book, a friend looked over the list of blunders I was tackling and asked me which one I thought was the biggest hindrance to the cause of Christ. I had to think about it for a while, but I finally chose this one. Not just for all the reasons I've listed above, but also because of something Jesus said in John 13:35: "Your love for one another will prove to the world that you are my disciples" (NLT). I take that to mean our love for one another legitimizes everything we do in the eyes of the lost. They still may not like us or agree with us, but if we're loving one another, at least they have to admit that we practice what we preach. However, when we're fussing and feuding, we come off looking like frauds. And that, it seems to me, is the biggest hindrance of all.

CREATING A CULTURE OF CALM

Part of our problem is that we live in a culture of conflict. When I was a boy, divorces were very rare. You almost never heard about somebody being involved in a lawsuit. Terms such as "road rage" and "air rage" hadn't been invented because there was no need for them. And people were generally gracious. They didn't spew streams of curse words or make obscene gestures because someone happened to be driving a little too slow in the fast lane. They didn't run onto the field at ball games and attack athletes. And athletes didn't climb ten rows up into the stands to attack the fans!

Yes, it's a different world today. Almost everywhere you look there's tension and conflict. People's nerves are on edge. Like ticking bombs, they're ready at any moment to explode. And they're walking into our churches every Sunday!

It would be wonderful if something magical happened to them as soon as they stepped across the threshold. It would be great if all their anger and frustration suddenly melted away like an April snowflake. But that's not what happens. People who are rude and contentious at home or at work are going to march into our churches with those same tendencies.

That's why it's imperative that we create a culture of calm in the church. No, we'll never be able to eliminate all conflict. As the old saying goes, people are like porcupines . . . we *need* one another, but sometimes we *needle* one another. True enough. But we can still create an environment that isn't conflict-friendly. Just as buildings are constructed with nonflammable materials and equipped with sprinkler systems and fire extinguishers, so we can create a fellowship that naturally suppresses conflict.

The question is, how?

It's all a matter of establishing the right priorities. Let me mention seven that will almost certainly do the trick.

PRIORITY #1: OBEY LEADERS. Hebrews 13:17 says, "Obey your spiritual leaders and do what they say. Their work is to watch over your souls, and they know they are accountable to God" (NLT). A command like this is rooted in the simple fact that all churches have people at every level of spiritual maturity. There will be brand-new baby Christians, backsliding Christians, hot and cold Christians, lukewarm Christians, and seasoned, mature Christians. God intends for some of those seasoned, mature Christians who are qualified to be moved into positions of leadership and for everyone else to submit to their authority.

In the Bible, such leaders are called elders, overseers, or pastors, and it's interesting to note that several of the qualifications they must meet uniquely qualify them for the work of conflict suppression. According to 1 Timothy 3:2–3, they are to be self-controlled, nonviolent, gentle, and peace loving. In other words, they should be the kind of guys who have a natural gift for calming and soothing.

But in the end, it won't matter how righteous and committed the elders are if no one pays any attention to them. So if you want to do something great for your church, show respect to your leaders and encourage others to do the same. You probably won't agree with every decision they make, but where in this world can you go where you would? And if the decision doesn't violate any biblical principle or precept, it's just a matter of opinion anyway. One of the most telling signs of spiritual maturity is when you're able to say, "I don't particularly care for this decision, but for the sake of harmony, I'm going to get on board and support it."

PRIORITY #2: CONFRONT TROUBLEMAKERS. Yes, the elders are supposed to be self-controlled, nonviolent, gentle, and peace loving, but that doesn't mean they're supposed to be wimps. On the contrary, they must have the courage to take decisive action when trouble arises.

One of the reasons the Corinthian church became such a hotbed of conflict and turmoil is because blatant sinners and troublemakers weren't dealt with. Look at Paul's heated words in 1 Corinthians 5:1–2:

> I can hardly believe the report about the sexual immorality going on among you, something so evil that even the pagans don't do it. I am told that you have a man in your church who is living in sin with his father's wife. And you are so proud of yourselves! Why aren't you mourning in sorrow and shame? *And why haven't you removed this man from your fellowship?* (NLT, emphasis added)

Clearly, Paul was upset that a man in the church was behaving so badly. But he was even more disappointed that the leaders hadn't dealt with him.

I suppose the man wasn't confronted for the same reason a lot of troublemakers aren't confronted in churches today. Confrontation is hard. It's an emotional, gut-wrenching experience. And it's fraught with uncertainty. You never know if the person is going to humbly repent or throw a kicking, screaming fit. In my experience, the results have been about fifty-fifty. But in almost every case, the church benefited from our decisive action. If the troublemaker didn't repent, he often left the church, which also solved the problem.

I'm going to address this issue in greater detail in chapter 9, but I'd like to add a word of caution here. There is a biblical way to confront troublemakers, and wise church leaders will follow that pattern to the letter. The core of that pattern is found in Titus 3:10: "If anyone is causing divisions among you, give a first and second warning. After that, have nothing more to do with the person" (NLT). Because the goal is always to persuade the troublemaker to repent, you don't just boot him out of the church immediately. Instead, you plead and reason with him. Sometimes a person just needs a little time to work through whatever issues are causing his bad behavior. By being patient, you can often salvage a brother. But if, after a second warning, there is no repentance, then the person must be removed from the body.

PRIORITY #3: REFUTE HERESY. One of the oldest causes of division in the church is false doctrine. Paul was speaking to the elders of the Ephesian church when he said, "I know full well that false teachers, like vicious wolves, will come in among you after I leave, not sparing the flock. Even some of you will distort the truth in order to draw a following" (Acts 20:29–30 NLT). The key phrase there is "in order to draw a following." Paul is not talking about the honest misunderstanding or misinterpretation of Scripture by people who mean well (though that can be a problem, too). He's talking about the intentional twisting of biblical truth by power-hungry people who have their own agendas.

Today, we really have to be on the lookout for heresy because of the proliferation of religions. On a given Sunday, new people from a dozen different religious backgrounds can walk through our doors, bringing who knows what ideas with them. And you can be sure that some of those people will be aggressive types who are searching for a place to wield influence.

That's why church leaders must be well-versed in the Scriptures and closely monitor any teaching that is done in the body. Too often, people are put into positions of leadership simply because they're good ol' boys and not because they're capable of discerning false doctrine. I've seen it a thousand times. Joe Blow has only a sixth-grade education and can't read worth a hoot, but he's the nicest guy you'd ever want to meet . . . so let's make him an elder!

I'm ashamed to admit that I'd been in the ministry for years before I fully understood Paul's insistence that an elder be "able to teach" (1 Timothy 3:2 NLT). I now realize that he didn't lay down that requirement because he was concerned about a shortage of teachers in the Sunday school. Rather, he was saying that elders must be on the same level with the teachers in the church when it comes to basic intellect, Bible knowledge, and discernment. Otherwise, slick false teachers would forever be able to pull the wool over their eyes.

PRIORITY #4: MEET NEEDS. Human nature dictates that we will be at our crankiest when we have unmet needs. I, for example, am perfectly charming 99 percent of the time. But Marilyn will tell you that when I'm hungry or extremely tired I can be a little out of sorts.

This is nothing new. In Acts 6 we find the story of some church widows who were being neglected in the daily distribution of food. Naturally, they started complaining, and I don't blame them. I start getting bent out of shape if the pizza delivery boy is ten minutes late! I can only imagine how I'd feel if my meals weren't showing up at all!

To their credit, the apostles set in motion a plan to see that the widows' needs were met. They didn't do it themselves, but they wisely delegated the job to seven men who were well respected and "full of the Holy Spirit and wisdom" (Acts 6:3 NLT), which enabled them to continue devoting themselves to preaching and prayer. And never again in Scripture do we hear about that same problem arising. What could have turned into a divisive church squabble was permanently laid to rest simply by getting organized to meet some simple needs.

Today, when a problem arises in the church, wise leaders will ask a few simple questions: Is this problem being caused by an unmet need? Are people complaining because they're hurting? Have we allowed some people to fall through the cracks of our ministry system? I would estimate that at least half the complaints I've heard over the years have been fixable with a little greater commitment to ministry, or at least a little better organization.

PRIORITY #5: SUPPRESS LEGALISM. For years I tried to explain legalism to people using highfalutin words and phrases. Then one day I heard it described as "spiritual nit-picking," and I've been using that definition ever since. If you've ever had a boss or a coach or a spouse "pick you apart" and find fault with every little thing you do, then you understand what a dispiriting thing legalism is. Not to mention irritating. It's what Jesus was accusing the Pharisees of when He told them that they crushed people "with impossible religious demands" (Matthew 23:4 NLT).

I'm sure you don't need a doctorate in sociology to know that anytime one group of people is crushing another group of people, you've got all the ingredients for a good scrap. Sooner or later, the *crushees* are going to get their fill of the *crushers*, and war is going to break out. That's why Jesus worked so hard to promote the gracious treatment of others through both His words and His actions. Luke 4:22 says, "All who were there spoke well of him and were amazed by the gracious words that fell from his lips" (NLT). And Matthew 9:10 tells us that Jesus was invited to dine with notorious sinners

. . . and accepted! Obviously, He did these things hoping we would follow His example. And follow it we must if we want to have peace in our churches.

We must preach grace and model kindness. While never winking at sin, we must be tenderhearted and understanding toward those who struggle in their faith and haven't yet overcome all the bad habits they picked up in the world. And we must make sure that our expectations of baby Christians are reasonable, giving them adequate time to grow into the faith that is second nature to those of us who were privileged to grow up in strong Christian homes.

One thing is certain. When people in our churches who are a little different or a little less than perfect start to be amazed at the gracious words that fall from our lips, we will have struck a mighty blow against legalism and taken a giant step toward peace and harmony.

PRIORITY #6: DISCOURAGE ARGUMENTS. Titus 3:9 says, "Do not get involved in foolish discussions about spiritual pedigrees or in quarrels and fights about obedience to Jewish laws. These kinds of things are useless and a waste of time" (NLT). And, I might add, they're dangerous. Why? Because when a person feels he's losing an argument, he will be tempted to drop a nuke. He'll be tempted to say or do something over the top to salvage his pride or, if nothing else, just to inflict pain. How many times have you turned on the news and watched a report about a fatal stabbing or shooting, then heard the reporter explain that it all started with an argument? Arguments always seem to lead to bad places.

However, I want to be quick to point out that not all disagreements are arguments and not all discussions are foolish.

Sometimes our consciences will demand that we engage in a spirited debate. That's all a part of defending the faith. But as Peter says, we must do this in a "gentle and respectful way" (1 Peter 3:16 NLT). We must never allow our words to turn into warheads.

It's a cliché, but it's true that it takes two to tango. It takes two people to have an argument. So let me challenge you to be quick to pull the plug on any discussion that looks as though it's about to turn in a dangerous direction. Even if you have to swallow your pride and forfeit the debate, go ahead and wave the white flag. Turn and walk away. By doing so you could not only salvage a friendship, you could spare the entire congregation a major trauma.

PRIORITY #7: FORGIVE SINNERS. If I could use only one Bible verse to promote church health and harmony, it would be Ephesians 4:32. Paul said, "Be kind to each other, tenderhearted, forgiving one another, just as God through Christ has forgiven you" (NLT).

Forgiveness is important for three reasons.

Number one, it is the proverbial bucket of cold water that douses a spark of controversy before it can explode into a roaring flame. If someone says something rude to you, don't snap back or stomp off in a huff, muttering under your breath. Just blow it off. Forgive the person and move on. Tell yourself that there's probably a behind-the-scenes reason why he or she was irritable or upset. Remind yourself that you, too, have made the same mistake. Think about how many times you've needed other people to cut you some slack.

The second reason why forgiveness is important is because sinners can't be restored and given another chance without it. I'll be honest and say that, at least in my experience, most hardcore troublemakers never change; they just hop from church to church.

But a few do change. I've seen some pretty nasty people grow out of their childish ways and become positive, supportive church members. But it never happens unless the people they've butted heads with are willing to let bygones be bygones.

And the third reason why forgiveness is important is because it makes us more like Jesus. Notice how Paul said, ". . . forgiving one another, *just as God through Christ has forgiven you*" (Ephesians 4:32 NLT, emphasis added). There are things we do in the church that make us visible. There are things we do that make us grow. There are things we do that make us efficient. But none of those things necessarily make us like Christ. Forgiveness does. I once heard a preacher say that we are never more like Jesus than when we give. I think he missed nailing the truth by three letters. I believe we are never more like Jesus than when we *for*give.

I want to wrap up this chapter by showing you something you may never have noticed in the book of Revelation. In the first few verses of Revelation 2, we find a letter from the Lord to the church at Ephesus. In that letter, He delivers a stinging rebuke:

> I have this complaint against you. You don't love me or each other as you did at first! (v. 4 NLT)

We always seem to focus on the words "you don't love me." But notice the additional phrase "or each other." Apparently, the church had lost (or was losing) the harmonious spirit it once possessed. People who once got along very well were evidently bickering. Relationships were fractured. People weren't speaking to one another. Maybe their fellowship didn't yet resemble a pay-per-view

Wrestlemania extravaganza, but it was apparently heading in that direction.

It's what the Lord said next that is chilling:

> Turn back to me again and work as you did at first. If you don't, I will come and remove your lampstand from its place among the churches. (v. 5 NLT)

It's that phrase "work as you did at first" that intrigues me. What kind of work had they gotten away from?

Apparently, the work of love.

If you're married, I don't have to tell you what the "work of love" is. It's what you have to fall back on during those times when you'd rather wear sandpaper underwear for a week than be in the same room with your spouse for five seconds. It's what you resort to when your Cinderella starts acting more like an ugly stepsister . . . or when your handsome prince starts resembling the frog your mother tried to tell you he was in the first place. The work of love is what holds marriages, friendships, and even churches together when they would otherwise come flying apart at the seams. It's what is required to build and maintain a culture of calm.

All seven of my points in the last section of this chapter were verb-driven:

- □ *Obey* leaders.
- □ *Confront* troublemakers.
- □ *Refute* heresy.
- □ *Meet* needs.
- □ *Suppress* legalism.

□ *Discourage* arguments.

□ *Forgive* sinners.

I believe these actions represent the work Jesus was referring to in His letter to the Ephesians. And after all these years, they're still the actions that are needed to build and maintain harmony in the church. Let me challenge you to look through the list and see which of these priorities you could contribute to in your church. If you're not in a leadership role, there may be some of these things you'll need to leave to others. But even if you're just getting started in the fellowship, you can obey leaders, help meet needs, and so on. Every little contribution helps.

It's late at night, and I'm sitting in my office with the official membership record of our church open before me. I recognize most of the names, having been the pastor here for so many years. But now my eyes are focused on a name that brings sadness to my heart. The name belongs to a person who is long gone from our family and that I have heard is no longer walking with God. My sadness is made greater by my memory of what happened.

That person was a victim of friendly fire.

I remember the incident well. It was unspeakably ugly. Several people got hurt. I feel a little sick just thinking about it.

And suddenly I wonder . . . *If I feel this bad, how must God feel?* Please.

Let's stop fighting among ourselves.

And knuckle down and do the work of love.

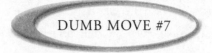

Missing Golden Opportunities

Thou shalt not be a victim.
Thou shalt not be a perpetrator.
Above all, thou shalt not be a bystander.

—HOLOCAUST MUSEUM,
WASHINGTON, D.C.

I'm kicking myself!

I was standing in one of Orlando's largest Christian bookstores, quietly browsing, when I heard someone speak my name. I glanced to my right and saw the special order desk about fifteen feet away. A man had asked the salesclerk if he had any copies of my book *The Samson Syndrome* in stock. He said his church's men's group was going to study the book and needed fifteen copies. (Did I mention what a fine-looking, intelligent, and cultured gentleman he was?)

Anyway, we've all said, "I'd love to be a fly on the wall . . ."
Meaning we'd love to be able to watch a situation unfold without
anyone knowing we were watching. Well, suddenly, I was that fly.
Neither the customer nor the salesclerk knew the author of the
book they were discussing was standing fifteen feet away. *Cool! I'm
just going to watch and see how this plays out!*

As I pretended to scan the shelves, the salesclerk tapped some
keys on the computer and learned that some copies of the book
were indeed in stock. Then he led the man to the very shelf where
I was browsing. We were only about five feet apart. They found
five copies of the book and then entered into a discussion about
what the price would be if the customer bought fifteen of them.
Meanwhile, I stood there thinking what a bizarre situation I was
in and wondering what the man would say if I stepped over and
introduced myself. I was just about to find out when he plucked
his cell phone off his belt and made a call. Not wanting to inter-
rupt, I held my ground and listened.

I gathered from his half of the conversation that he was the
men's ministry leader for his church and that he was calling his
pastor for advice. Should he buy the five books and special-order
ten more? Or buy the five books and check with some other stores
in town to see if he could find ten more? And should he pay full
price or look elsewhere for a store that might give a discount?

Suddenly, a jolt of guilt shot through me. I was eavesdropping!
Or was I? I wasn't sure. I was still standing in the same spot I'd been
in when I first heard my name. I hadn't taken one step out of my
way to hear anything. On the other hand, I was only pretending to
look at the books in front of me. I was actually straining my ears
to the limits of their ability, hanging on every word the man was

saying. Would he think of me as an eavesdropper if I suddenly stepped forward and introduced myself? Or would he be happy to meet me? As I stood there weighing these questions, the man did the one thing I wasn't expecting. While still talking on his phone, he walked out of the store without buying a single book!

And I've been kicking myself ever since.

I keep thinking about all the nice things that could have happened if I had stepped up and introduced myself when I first heard my name. I might have made a new friend. I most certainly would have learned what wonderful, enlightened, deeply spiritual church was planning to study my book. And who knows, I might have been asked to speak to their men's group. Looking back, I can't help thinking God put a great opportunity right in front of me. To use baseball imagery, He threw me a fat one right down the middle . . . and I stood there and watched it go by!

I'm guessing it wouldn't be very hard for you to think back to a time when you missed a golden opportunity, too. Maybe your next-door neighbors suffered a death in the family and you could have dropped by with a pot of homemade soup or a casserole as a way of sharing the love of Jesus . . . but you didn't. Or maybe one of your coworkers came dragging in last Monday morning with a hangover and a load of guilt, and you had a perfect opportunity to tell him about a better way of life . . . but you didn't. Or maybe your church was recruiting helpers for some short-staffed ministries, and you could have signed up . . . but you didn't.

I cringe when I think about how many golden opportunities to make an impact for Christ are missed by God's people every single day—and how much good is left undone by those missed opportunities. For example, let's say that each of the five hundred members of a single church misses one opportunity to advance the cause of Christ per day. In just one year, that would be 182,500 blown opportunities! I can't imagine what that would mean in terms of hurting people who could have been comforted, confused people who could have been given direction, discouraged people who could have been given hope, burdened people who could have been given relief, hungry people who could have been given something to eat, or, most of all, lost people who could have been told about Jesus. Let's be super-conservative and say that just 10 percent of those opportunities would have borne fruit for the kingdom. That doesn't sound like much, but it's still 18,250 productive efforts that were forever lost!

By the way, in case you're wondering if I'm overestimating the problem, consider that churches are closing at a rate of thirty-five hundred to six thousand per year. Twenty-five thousand churches in a recent year didn't report a single baptism. And only 3 percent of professing Christians have ever led anyone to Christ.[1] Would numbers like that be on the books if we were actively seizing opportunities to build the kingdom?

Nowadays, we put an incredible amount of emphasis on church leadership and structure. We organize campaigns and programs that are designed to lift the church to new heights. And I'm in favor these things. I've been to the conferences and participated in the programs, and they are helpful. But sometimes I wonder if we haven't overlooked and undervalued those moments that can't be structured or fit into a program. I'm talking about the countless mundane moments of life when, out of the blue, an opportunity suddenly materializes. At the grocery store, the Little League game, the PTA meeting, the gas pump, or the bank window. I'm talking about those moments when neither your pastor nor your dog-eared copy of *The Purpose Driven Life* are available for consultation, but you have an opportunity to make a difference with a well-chosen word or action . . . if you act immediately.

A CASE STUDY

There are many Bible stories that give us vivid pictures of people both missing and seizing opportunities to advance the cause of Christ. The parable of the Good Samaritan might be the best-known. But my favorite comes from the early days of the church:

As for Philip, an angel of the Lord said to him, "Go south down the desert road that runs from Jerusalem to Gaza" (v. 26). So he did, and he met the treasurer of Ethiopia, a eunuch of great authority under the queen of Ethiopia. The eunuch had gone to Jerusalem to worship, and he was now returning. Seated in his carriage, he was reading aloud from the book of the prophet Isaiah.

The Holy Spirit said to Philip, "Go over and walk along beside the carriage" (v. 29).

Philip ran over and heard the man reading from the prophet Isaiah, so he asked, "Do you understand what you are reading?" (v. 30).

The man replied, "How can I, when there is no one to instruct me?" (v. 30). And he begged Philip to come up into the carriage and sit with him. The passage of Scripture he had been reading was this:

He was led as a sheep to the slaughter.

And as a lamb is silent before the shearers,

he did not open his mouth.

He was humiliated and received no justice.

Who can speak of his descendants?

For his life was taken from the earth. (Acts 8:32–34 NLT)

As they rode along, they came to some water, and the eunuch said, "Look! There's some water! Why can't I be baptized?" (v. 36). He ordered the carriage to stop, and they went down into the water, and Philip baptized him (see Acts 8:26–38 NLT).

I see five practical lessons in this passage:

LESSON #1: SOME OPPORTUNITIES, IF THEY ARE MISSED, WILL BE LOST FOREVER. Because they came from different parts of the world, it's more than likely that this was the only time Philip's life intersected with the Ethiopian's. If, for any reason, he had failed to initiate this conversation, the Ethiopian would have gone on his way and might never have found someone to teach him the good news. Likewise, there will be people you and I will come into contact with only one time. We'll have one shot to make a difference.

Recently, Marilyn and I attended a spring training baseball game between the Cardinals and the Astros. After the second inning, there was a downpour that sent all the fans scurrying for cover. I found myself standing under a protective ledge next to a guy who was wearing a Cardinals cap. Since I was wearing one, too (and since we were in the Astros's home park), I used it as a starting point for a conversation. Come to find out, he was visiting Florida from St. Louis and was a former pastor. As the conversation progressed, I learned that he had gotten out of the ministry because of discouragement. For about twenty minutes, we stood shoulder to shoulder in a crowd of baseball fans (with wind and water whipping all around) and talked about our faith and the calling we both felt God had placed on our lives. He seemed to have regrets, and I tried my best to encourage him. Finally, we shook hands and went our separate ways. I'd be surprised if I ever see him again this side of heaven.

How much good did I do? I have no idea. Honestly, I doubt that he ran back to St. Louis and found himself a church to pastor. Just the same, I'm so glad I initiated that conversation. I can't get over the feeling that God brought us together at that brief moment in time for an eternal purpose.

Every morning, before you get too deep into your day, you need to ask God to open your eyes and help you recognize whatever divine appointments He has set up for you. They can come when you least expect them and be gone in a flash. The kingdom can be advanced or hindered depending on your readiness.

LESSON #2: GOD WILL GIVE SPECIAL OPPORTUNITIES TO THOSE WHO ARE COMMITTED AND PREPARED. There may have been other Christians in the vicinity, but it's clear that God chose Philip to talk to the Ethiopian. Did you notice that verse 35 says Philip used the Isaiah passage and "many others" to tell him the good news about Jesus? Philip's knowledge of the Scriptures was undoubtedly one of the major reasons why God tapped him on the shoulder and not someone else . . . which leads me to say something I've always believed. The single most important thing you can do to prepare yourself to be used by God is study the Scriptures. You need to study on your own, for sure. But you also need to listen to the Word preached, attend a regular Bible study, and read good, Bible-based books. You just never know when you're going to pick up an idea or an insight that will enable you to seize a golden opportunity.

I've always spent a good bit of time studying. (When you have to crank out a new sermon and a couple of fresh Bible studies every week, you don't have much choice.) Then, a few years ago, when God opened the door for me to start writing books, I started studying even more. What I've learned is that the more I study, the more opportunities to make a spiritual impact I seem to have. I marvel at how often I've stumbled across a profound truth one day and gotten a chance to use it in a conversation the very next day. Or sometimes the same day! It's as if God says, "Okay, Mark, I think you've grasped this concept. Now pay attention, because I'm going to send someone your way who needs to hear it."

Let me encourage you to renew your commitment to the Word. And to pay close attention when you're reading your Bible, studying with friends, or listening to your preacher on Sunday morning. At any moment, a truth could be spoken that God wants you to relay to someone like Philip's Ethiopian—someone you haven't met, but whom He's planning to send across your path.

LESSON #3: SOME OPPORTUNITIES ARE MUCH LARGER THAN THEY FIRST APPEAR. At first glance, Philip's opportunity was simply to share the gospel with another man. But a closer look reveals a potential of mind-boggling proportions. Remember, the Ethiopian was a man of great influence in his country. Imagine what could have happened (and probably did happen) when he arrived back home, bursting with excitement about Jesus. There's no telling how many people he witnessed to or how many he baptized, all because Philip seized an opportunity to initiate a conversation.

Another striking example of this truth is seen in Jesus' conversation with the Samaritan woman (see John 4:1–42). At high noon on a hot day in Samaria, He was seated beside Jacob's well, mopping sweat from His brow. When a woman from the local village came by to draw water, He asked her for a drink. I love the fact that He didn't say or do anything religious. He didn't say, "If you died tonight, do you know for sure that you'd go to heaven?" And He didn't pull a copy of *The Four Spiritual Laws* out from under His tunic and wave it in her face. He simply asked for a drink. But that was enough to trigger one of the most fascinating conversations in all of Scripture.

But it's what happened *after* the conversation that I'm most interested in here. The woman, having been profoundly touched by her conversation with the Messiah, ran home and started telling everyone she knew about Him:

> Many Samaritans from the village believed in Jesus because the woman had said, "He told me everything I ever did!" When they came out to see him, they begged him to stay at their village. So he stayed for two days, long enough for many of them to hear his message and believe. Then they said to the woman, "Now we believe because we have heard him ourselves, not just because of what you told us. He is indeed the Savior of the world." (John 4:39–42 NLT)

A one-on-one conversation that was started in a moment that could be described only as mundane ended up turning an entire village upside down. Clearly, you cannot know when you look at an opportunity what its potential is. That's why it's best to adopt the notion that there are no small or insignificant opportunities to advance the kingdom. Some may be bigger than others, but there are no small opportunities.

LESSON #4: SOME OPPORTUNITIES BEAR IMMEDIATE FRUIT FOR THE KINGDOM. Philip had barely finished telling the Ethiopian about Jesus when he spotted a body of water and asked if he could be baptized. Obviously, it doesn't always happen that way, but you might be surprised at how often it does. What we need to remember is that the world is full of frustrated, unhappy people. You probably rub shoulders with a dozen people every day who hate their lives and would be willing to try something different in a heartbeat . . . if they only knew what to try.

One time I witnessed to a woman who was not responsive at all. I got nowhere with her. But she did make a fascinating statement that I've never forgotten. She said, "You're too late. I went through my 'religion phase' a few years ago." When I asked what she meant, she said, "There was a time in my life when I gave religion a try, but the people I fell in with were all holier-than-thou wackos, and I couldn't take it. I decided it wasn't for me."

I wonder about three things every time I think about the woman's statement.

First, I wonder what might have happened if, during her "religion phase," she'd connected with some believers who weren't wackos.

Second, I wonder how many non-wacko believers missed golden opportunities to impact her life during that time when she was open to spiritual ideas and concepts.

And third, I wonder how many people there are close to me (and you) right now who are going through a "religion phase" . . . people who may not be advertising it, but who would be open to hearing what we have to say about the Lord. I'm guessing there are more than we realize. Probably a lot more.

LESSON #5: THE GOAL OF EVERY OPPORTUNITY SHOULD BE TO POINT PEOPLE TO JESUS. It would have been easy for Philip to fritter away his once-in-a-lifetime opportunity with the Ethiopian by talking about side issues. For example, politics would have made an interesting topic of discussion since the man was a high government official in his country. Or Philip's curiosity about the lifestyles of the rich and famous could have compelled him to ask what it was like being part of a queen's inner circle. But that's not what happened. Philip stayed on point and made Jesus the issue.

That doesn't mean we should be preaching at everybody we come into contact with. Some opportunities to advance the cause of Christ require very few words to be spoken . . . or perhaps none at all. For example, a cup of cold water offered to a thirsty beggar would likely not be accompanied by a theological dissertation. However, Colossians 3:17 says, "Whatever you do or say, let it be as a representative of the Lord Jesus" (NLT). When we make an attempt to advance the cause of Christ, we shouldn't be afraid to admit that's what we're doing. Whenever we can (and without being obnoxious about it), we need to let people know that we are servants of the Savior.

The story of Philip and the Ethiopian has always been one of my favorites. I just love how a saved person and a lost person rubbed shoulders on the busy highway of life, on an ordinary day, far from the nearest church, and when it was all over, another name was added to the Lamb's Book of Life (see Revelation 21:27). As I observe our dizzying obsession with church structures and programs, I wonder if we've forgotten that people can be saved and the kingdom can be built in such a simple, natural way.

WHY OPPORTUNITIES ARE SO EASY TO MISS

I don't know who invented stereograms, but if that person ever reads this book, I'd like for him (or her) to know that he (or she) has brought much pain and misery into my life. You know what a stereogram is, don't you? It's one of those blasted pictures that have images hidden in them. They're usually very colorful and have the look of abstract art, but if you look at them just right, you're supposed to see an image. My problem is that I can never see the image. I don't mean I have a hard time seeing it. I mean I have never, ever seen it. Not even once! I've been with friends who were marveling at the pretty sailboat while I stood there squinting and tilting my head, saying, "What sailboat? I don't see a sailboat!"

I recently learned that in order to see the hidden images you have to practice something called "parallel viewing." It was explained to me by a friend and sounded like something I might be able to do, so the next time I was on the Net I pulled up some stereograms. I was very excited, thinking I was finally going to have an experience that everyone else in the world had already had. But nothing happened. I still can't see the crazy things. Honestly, I'm starting to wonder if stereograms are a complete hoax and if I'm the only remaining adult on planet Earth who hasn't figured it out yet. I'm planning to ask my buddy next week when he takes me snipe hunting.

Unfortunately, spotting opportunities to advance the cause of Christ can also be very difficult. Like the hidden images in stereograms, they can be right in front of us, yet almost impossible to see. Let me suggest a few reasons for this:

We Have Our Own Hurts and Needs to Contend With

I have a friend who has some serious health problems that cause her a lot of pain. For the most part, she copes very well. But once in a while, when her discomfort is really intense, she has what she calls "a give-up day." For one day only, she allows herself to give up. She might curl into the fetal position and not even get out of bed. Most certainly she will whine and complain. Often she cries. Sometimes she screams. But only for a day. Then she gets back into the swing of things, even if it kills her. And sometimes it almost does.

Unfortunately, there are a good many people around who don't just have give-up days. They have give-up weeks, months, years, and even lives. They become professional wound lickers. All they can think about is how bad they have it. Not in a million years would it occur to them that someone nearby might have it just as bad, or even worse. A hundred needy people a day could pass them by, and they'd never notice.

People Are Great Actors

Another reason why we sometimes don't spot opportunities is because people are great actors. I, for example, have never taken an acting class, but I've snowed a lot of people on a lot of occasions.

There have been many Sunday mornings over the years that found me hurting and discouraged, but when I arrived at church I slapped a smile on my face and did my job without giving a hint of my true feelings. I've told hilarious jokes from the pulpit and had the whole congregation roaring with laughter on days when I felt so frustrated I wanted to resign. Even away from a weekend worship service, I often feel the need to act more upbeat around people than I really feel.

I think I must get this from my dad. The man has had cancer surgery, chemo, radiation, open-heart surgery, a stroke, and is a diabetic. But if you ever ask him how he's feeling, he'll nod and say, "Pretty good."

You see the point, don't you? For every person who wears his feelings on his sleeve, there will be one who keeps all of his problems and frustrations under wraps. He may be in desperate need of help or encouragement, but you'll have a hard time seeing it.

The Pace of Our Lives

A third reason why we sometimes fail to notice opportunities is because of the pace of our lives. When Marilyn and I go for a walk in our neighborhood, we notice everything. We talk about how people have their yards landscaped or the color schemes they've chosen for their houses. However, when we're driving we don't see as much detail. Mostly, we notice buildings and signs. And then when we fly, we notice even less. In fact, at thirty thousand feet, it's pretty hard to see anything.

Something similar happens as we live our lives from day to day. The faster the pace of our lives becomes, the less we notice. Not long ago, a woman I know served her husband with divorce papers. His response was, "I didn't even know we had a problem." The reason he didn't know was because he was working eighty hours a week. His wife had been having an affair for six months, and he didn't even notice.

So one of the biggest challenges we face is to become more aware of the opportunities around us. We need to take our eyes off ourselves. We need to look for subtle signs of distress in people who may be too proud or too afraid to admit they're struggling. And we need to slow down.

IT ALL BOILS DOWN TO PASSION

At this point, I'd like to say something to the reader who agrees in principle with the message of this chapter, but feels that he or she just isn't equipped to be much of an opportunity seizer. Maybe you're extremely shy. Maybe you're the kind of person who always thinks of the perfect thing to say about an hour after the opportunity has passed. Or maybe you're disabled, sick, or elderly, and you just don't enjoy much interaction with people. If so, I want you to read the following true story.

Greta was terminally ill—blind, in chronic pain, and hooked up to multiple drains, drips, and catheters. She'd suffered a stroke and couldn't speak. She communicated by blinking her eyes for yes or no. Yet in the last weeks of her life, she won a young nurse to Christ and led a volunteer who had wandered from the faith into a new and vibrant relationship with the Lord.

Impossible? Not at all. Because Greta asked the volunteer—

blink blink—to read to her every day from the Bible that was always on her bedside table. Reading from the living, active Word of God over those weeks fanned into flame again the faith that hospital volunteer thought she had squashed years ago. Soon she was sharing Christ with other terminal patients.

Greta also communicated by humming. She might not have been able to speak, but almost anytime you went by her room you could hear her humming the hymns from her Christian Reformed upbringing. Whenever the nurse went in to care for Greta, she had to listen. At first it irritated her, as the familiar words from the rejected faith of her parents played over and over in her head. But after a while, she began asking Greta, "Do you still believe all those promises of Jesus?" *Blink.* (Yes.) "Even with what God has let happen to you?" *Hard blink.* (Yes!) And so a young nurse was won to Christ by a sightless, speechless, dying Dutch woman.[2]

It's mind-boggling (and heartbreaking) to think that Greta probably did more to advance the cause of Christ in her dying days than the majority of believers who are blessed with perfect health do in a lifetime. Remember, I stated earlier that only 3 percent of confessing Christians have ever led someone to Christ. Yet she led two people to the Lord while being almost completely incapacitated!

Clearly, the secret to advancing the cause of Christ is not talent or ability. It's not youth, good health, or good looks. It's not even wit or intelligence.

It's passion.

It's believing with all your heart that people are lost without Jesus. It's caring so much about their souls that you never stop looking for opportunities to point them in His direction. It's being courageous enough to risk rejection. It's being willing to step out of the crowd and speak words that some will find offensive. It's believing, as Greta did, that the opportunities never stop coming, even up to the very end of your life. And it's believing, as Greta did, that even when you can't do much of anything, there's always *something* you can do.

When I first read Greta's story, I found myself wondering what would happen if even a few Christians in one place ever mustered up that kind of passion for the Lord. And then it hit me: I don't have to wonder. I *know* what would happen!

Because once upon a time, it did.

The book of Acts tells the story. Driven by their passion for the Lord, a handful of ordinary people seized every opportunity they got to tell someone about Him. Yes, they made some enemies. And yes, they suffered some as a result. But they also did something else worth noting: They turned the world upside down (see Acts 17:6).

We could debate long and hard about whether the world could ever again be turned upside down for Christ. My opinion is that such a discussion would be pointless. It seems to me that the far more important question is whether a church, a workplace, a family, or a neighborhood could be turned upside down for Christ. Most of us would surely agree that the answer to that question is a resounding "yes!"

So what are we waiting for?

The next time God throws you a big, fat opportunity right down the middle, don't just stand there and watch it go by.

Swing for the fences.

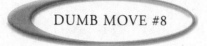

Settling for Mediocrity

I am a big believer in the "mirror test." All that matters is if
you can look in the mirror and honestly tell the person you see
there that you have done your best.

—JOHN MCKAY

When the people I work with pick up this book and read the
title of this chapter, I know they're going to roll their eyes and say,
"Oh, no! Here we go again!" You see, they constantly accuse me
of being a perfectionist. I always point out that they would never
say such a thing if they could see my sock drawer. But since they
haven't seen it, they continue to level that accusation against me
(in a good-natured way) every time I insist that we tighten up the
ship a little bit.

The truth is that I am *not* a perfectionist. I simply understand
the importance of making excellence a priority in the Lord's work.
And the reason I understand this is not because I'm so smart.
Rather, it's because I've worked in a variety of places—where

143

excellence was a priority and where it wasn't—and I can tell you that when it's missing, the Lord's work is hindered.

THE SLIPSHOD HALL OF FAME

To show you what I mean and to lay a foundation for this chapter, let me introduce you to what I lovingly call the "Slipshod Hall of Fame." The people I'm about to describe are fictitious, and yet, you'll find people just like them serving in churches all across America.

Jerry the Janitor

Jerry was unemployed when the church started looking for a janitor, so he applied for the job. He'd never been a janitor and never wanted to be a janitor. But the church needed a janitor and he needed a job, so everyone called the arrangement "a God thing."

The church leaders agreed to pay Jerry two hundred dollars a week to keep a twenty-thousand-square-foot building clean, which made Jerry the highest-paid person in town because most weeks he was able to do the entire job in about twenty minutes. His idea of cleaning the restroom was to walk in, flush the toilet, empty the wastebasket, and spray a little Lysol in the air to cover up the odor. Fifteen seconds flat. Maybe twenty for a two-holer.

Willie the Worship Leader

Willie loves music. Thirty-five years ago, he played the lead in the local high school's production of *Oklahoma*. Since then he's had what he calls "a nice little career in show business," singing at weddings and funerals in three counties. Willie isn't the greatest singer in the world, but his friends are quick to point out that what he lacks in ability, he makes up for in volume and enthusiasm.

Occasionally, Willie gets inspired and decides it's time for the congregation to learn a new song. Of course, Willie's idea of a new song is any song he doesn't know. It may be a dirge that was written two hundred years ago, but if he hasn't heard it, it's new.

Sarah the Soloist

Sarah never met a high note she didn't like. She never met one she could hit, either, but that doesn't stop her from trying, usually on the final note of a grand finale. She takes great comfort from the fact that every time she finishes a song, the congregation bursts into raucous applause. What she doesn't realize is that the people are clapping because the song is over and the pain has stopped.

Pearl the Pianist

Pearl is a fine lady who's been the church pianist for forty-five years. Other gifted pianists have come through the church during that time, but since Pearl and her husband donated the piano in 1972, none of them have ever gotten a chance to play.

Pearl's problem is that she has one volume (loud) and one speed (fast). Consequently, everything she plays comes out sounding like a John Philip Sousa march. A visiting musician once marveled at her ability to make "Sweet Hour of Prayer" sound just like "Stars and Stripes Forever."

Gary and Gwen the Greeters

Gary and Gwen love God. They love the church. They love their preacher. They just don't love each other . . . at least not on

Sunday mornings. That always seems to be the time they get into a fight. It might have something to do with the fact that Gwen struggles to get herself and their three preschoolers ready while Gary sits on the sofa reading the sports page, yelling, "What's taking so long?" every five minutes.

By the time they finally get to their posts, they're both angry and sour-faced. One morning a sweet little old lady smiled and said, "Isn't it a beautiful morning?" Gwen angrily shoved a bulletin at the woman and said, "I've seen better."

Larry the Lawn Mower

Good ol' Larry loves to work outdoors. He loves the smell of fresh grass clippings. He can bounce for hours on the seat of a John Deere and never get bored. The problem is, he does all of his mowing and trimming on Monday. By the time Sunday rolls around, the church grounds look shaggy and neglected.

Let me hasten to add that all these members of the Slipshod Hall of Fame are good people. No one is challenging their faith, their sincerity, or their salvation. In some cases, they may even be doing the best they can. My point is simply that the church needs to be more conscious of the way it presents itself to the lost. It's true, God never said, "Go ye into all the world and impress people." But you can't go anywhere in the world and find a business or organization that is thriving on mediocrity. Why would we think the church is an exception?

As I was researching this chapter, I asked about two dozen people a question: "What's the first thing that comes to your mind when you hear the word *excellence*?" I got a variety of answers:

- Lance Armstrong (He'd just won the Tour de France *again*.)
- Walt Disney World (The happiest place on earth.)
- The New England Patriots (They'd just won the Super Bowl *again*.)
- Krispy-Kreme Doughnuts (No comment needed.)
- Wal-Mart (Taking the world, one superstore at a time.)
- The Bible (A perennial best seller.)
- God (The most popular answer.)

What's interesting (and sad) is that no one said, "The church." When we hear the word *excellence*, we think of God, the Bible, and all sorts of secular businesses, celebrities, and sports teams, but, apparently, we don't think of the church. Surely, that fact is a source of great frustration to God.

WHY EXCELLENCE MATTERS

I know a lot of people would say I'm making a mountain out of a molehill. Every time Christians are talking and the subject of excellence comes up, you can bet somebody will say, "It doesn't really matter if things are done perfectly, as long as our hearts are right. After all, we're not professionals." And there is truth in that statement. However, it's a very short step from there to mediocrity. I've noticed that most of the people who blurt out a comment like that are contenders for membership in the Slipshod Hall of Fame. Whenever you speak the words "it doesn't really matter" in any context, you're probably already heading downhill.

Let me tell you why excellence *does* really matter:

God Loves Excellence

First, it matters because God loves it. We know He loves excellence because everything about Him bears its mark.

Like His creation, for example. Genesis 1:31 says, "Then God looked over all he had made, and he saw that it was excellent in every way" (NLT). If you've ever had your breath taken away by a spectacular sunset or driven through the Smokies in the fall or been bowled over by a frothy wave on a hot summer day, you've experienced firsthand the excellence of God's creation.

And then there's His character. Psalm 145:17 says, "The LORD is righteous in everything he does; he is filled with kindness" (NLT). You and I might be righteous out of fear. We might be afraid that if we don't behave, we'll get in trouble. But who would God have to answer to if He decided to break a few rules? If anyone could compromise his integrity without fear, it would be the One who wrote the rules in the first place! Even so, He is righteous in all He does. His integrity never wavers.

And what about His commands? Romans 7:12 says, "The law itself is holy and right and good" (NLT). What God gave us in the Bible is the perfect plan for joy-filled living. Even the world knows this. Go to the self-help section of any secular bookstore and thumb through the pages of the bestsellers. You'll probably run across some pretty wacky ideas, but you'll also find a surprising number of biblical principles sprinkled in among them. The authors may not acknowledge them as such, but that's exactly what they are.

And we can't forget His faithfulness. In Hebrews 13:5, He said, "I will never fail you. I will never forsake you" (NLT). If you've ever been abandoned by your friends when you were in trouble . . . or if your spouse has ever packed up and left without warning . . . or if you are the parent of a prodigal son or daughter, you know the beauty of this promise.

Do you see what I mean? God obviously loves excellence, and that's reason enough for us to love it, too.

The Bible Commands Excellence

The second reason why excellence matters is because the Bible commands it. If I tried to tell you that baptism is unimportant, you'd grab your Bible and show me I was mistaken. If I tried to tell you the Lord's Supper was a waste of time, you'd grab your Bible and correct me in no time flat. Or if I dared to suggest that faithfulness in marriage is highly overrated, you'd grab your Bible and preach me a dandy sermon.

Why, then, do we allow people to get away with saying that excellence isn't important? Have we forgotten that it, too, is commanded in Scripture? Colossians 3:23 says, "Work hard and cheerfully at whatever you do, as though you were working for the Lord rather than for people" (NLT). But beyond that, the Bible instructs us to:

- Give generously (see 2 Corinthians 8:7).
- Speak truthfully (see Ephesians 4:25).
- Work diligently (see 2 Thessalonians 3:12).
- Suffer patiently (see James 5:7–8).
- Interact peacefully (see Romans 12:18).
- Worship regularly (see Hebrews 10:25).
- Forgive completely (see Ephesians 4:32).
- Think positively (see Philippians 4:8).
- Love completely (see Ephesians 5:25).

- ☐ Choose wisely (see Ephesians 5:15).
- ☐ Live quietly (see 1 Thessalonians 4:11).

What do all these things add up to if not a life of excellence? It's high time we realized that nothing is more clearly and frequently commanded in Scripture than excellence. Not baptism. Not the Lord's Supper. *Nothing!*

People Respond to Excellence

The third reason why excellence matters is because people respond to it. Here in central Florida, we have two perfect illustrations. One would be Walt Disney World. Forty million people a year show up to see Mickey and his friends. The reason is because Disney does everything with excellence. People know that if they see a show on Disney property, it will be worth telling their friends about. They know that if they get on a Disney thrill ride, it will scare their socks off. They know that if they eat a Disney hot dog, it will taste as good or better than any hot dog they've ever had. Everyone talks about how expensive Disney is, but people just keep paying the money no matter how high the prices get because they know they're getting the best.

On the flip side, central Florida is also home to the Tampa Bay Devil Rays. Every night they play in front of tens of thousands of empty seats. They try all sorts of promotions in an effort to draw a crowd, but nothing works. Why? Because they're lousy. Because they lose almost every night. Because they're always in last place. But mark my words. If, by some miracle, they ever put a championship-caliber team on the field, those seats will have bodies in them. People respond to excellence.

And so it is in the church.

Right now, think about the fastest-growing church in your community. I will guarantee you that it's doing some things better than any other church in town. It may be offering better music, better preaching, better youth programs . . . I don't know what. But in some area (or probably several areas) that church has elevated its game and word is getting around.

Years ago I heard about two churches on separate sides of a very small town. They were very much alike and both had about thirty worshippers on a typical Sunday. But then, suddenly, one of the churches had about fifty worshippers and the other was down to ten. What happened? One of the churches decided to pave its parking lot. The people in that little town realized that if they worshipped at the church with the paved parking lot, they wouldn't have to tromp through the mud in their Sunday shoes on rainy mornings.

Now, you can shake your head and say those people were pretty shallow for changing churches just to keep their shoes clean. Or you can nod your head and say that church was pretty smart for being the first to pave its parking lot. Both statements are probably true, but the point is, people respond to excellence. They always have, and they always will.

We live in a time when people are very careful when it comes to choosing the church they want to attend. No longer do people blindly choose a church simply because they were raised in one just like it. People are more willing than ever to shop around, especially when they move to a new community. We all need to realize—like it or not—that we'll probably get one chance to make a good impression. If what people see and experience when they walk through our doors is slipshod and disorganized, we likely will never see them again. And who knows, we may have soured them on the church once and for all. Imagine the cumulative effect on the kingdom if thousands of churches across the country are making the same mistake!

WHAT EXCELLENCE REQUIRES

In the 1967 World Series, Bob Gibson, of the St. Louis Cardinals, set a standard for postseason pitching excellence that has never been matched. In the hotly contested seven-game series against the Boston Red Sox, Gibson won all three of his starts and finished with three complete games, one shutout, a 1.00 earned run average, and 26 strikeouts in 27 innings. He even hit a home run in the fifth inning of the seventh game for good measure. Since 1967 some of the game's greatest pitchers have taken the mound in postseason play. Tom Seaver, Roger Clemens, Greg Maddux, Randy Johnson, and Pedro Martinez have all had their shot, but no one has been able to match Gibson's performance. Tim McCarver, now a broadcaster, was Gibson's catcher during those glory years. He has often joked, "Bob Gibson is the luckiest pitcher I ever saw. He always pitched when the other team didn't score any runs!"

Obviously, Bob Gibson wasn't lucky. No individual, team, business, or church that achieves remarkable success is ever just lucky. We may tell ourselves that to make our own failures easier to swallow, but it's never true. Excellence is intentional. It happens when people make a conscious choice to meet its requirements. Let me mention five qualities that excellence, especially as it relates to our kingdom responsibilities, will always require:

Courage

First, excellence will require courage. One of my favorite places to visit in Florida is Silver Springs. It's not as high-tech or glitzy as Disney World, but its natural beauty is breathtaking, and its many exhibits and excursions are very educational. On a recent visit, my wife and I learned about the park's commitment to rehabilitating injured birds of prey, such as hawks and eagles. But I wondered, how does an eagle, the most majestic and powerful of all birds, get injured? Usually in one of two ways. Either it flies into something, such as a power line, an antenna, or an airplane; or it is the victim of a gunshot wound.

Christians who are committed to the pursuit of excellence in their churches face similar dangers. There are many obstacles that can be "flown into" along the way, such as apathy, a lack of funds, or small faith. But there are also shotgun-toting lovers of the status quo who view any disruption of their comfort zone as a personal attack. If you get serious about trying to upgrade a floundering ministry in your church, you are more than likely to come under verbal fire from a trigger-happy traditionalist who isn't about to give up his sacred cow without a fight.

Many Christians have recognized the need for change in their churches, and even longed for it, but declined to pursue it because they knew it couldn't be accomplished without a fair amount of boat-rocking and feather-ruffling. In essence, they chose shallow harmony over effectiveness.

However, it should be pointed out that the great heroes of the Bible never made peace their primary objective. Jesus, for example, earned a reputation as a troublemaker because He kept upsetting the status quo and challenging people to elevate their thinking and

153

their morality. And His disciples, when they were threatened and ordered to stop talking to people about Jesus, said, "We cannot stop telling about the wonderful things we have seen and heard" (Acts 4:20 NLT).

Personally, I have never regretted choosing excellence over peace. When my daughter was small, our wills collided on a regular basis. At the age of two, she failed to see the wisdom behind my instructions and prohibitions and demonstrated that failure with spirited challenges to my authority. However, she was such a cute little thing that it was tempting for me to let her have her way. That pouty bottom lip and those little tearstained cheeks were almost more than I could take. But in the end, I made excellence, not peace, my priority. Now she's in her twenties and a daughter any father could be proud of. I'm so glad I chose to "disturb the peace" when her behavior was less than excellent.

Right now, if you're involved in a slipshod ministry at your church, I challenge you to buckle your chinstrap and make 2 Timothy 1:7 your motto: "For God has not given us a spirit of fear and timidity, but of power, love, and self-discipline" (NLT). Excellence requires courage.

Giftedness

Second, excellence requires giftedness. Read the following passage very carefully:

> God has given gifts to each of you from his great variety of spiritual gifts. Manage them well so that God's generosity can flow through you. Are you called to be a speaker? Then speak as though God himself were speaking through you. Are you called to help

others? Do it with all the strength and energy that God supplies. Then God will be given glory in everything through Jesus Christ. (1 Peter 4:10–11 NLT)

One of the greatest obstacles to excellence in the church is the mismanagement of God's gifts. Too many people are not serving in their areas of giftedness. There are three ways this can happen.

For one thing, some people have no idea what their gifts are. It might be because they've never thought about it. Or it might be because they've been lied to. Yes, we do lie to one another in church, especially when it comes to our service. Just let a woman stand up and sing a song off-pitch, and I will guarantee you a dozen people will tell her she did a great job. Obviously, they're trying to be kind and encouraging, but the end result is that the woman walks away thinking people enjoy her singing!

Also, some people know what their gifts are but refuse to serve in that area. For example, a gifted schoolteacher might say, "I teach all week long, and I don't want to have to teach on Sundays, too. I need a break from teaching."

And finally, some people know what gifts they lack but insist on serving in those areas anyway. I visited a church one time where the Sunday school teacher had a severe stuttering problem. He was very sincere and I could tell he was a terrific person, but I found myself hopelessly distracted by his impediment. I also noticed that the classroom was practically empty. When I asked the pastor about the situation, his response was telling. He said, "The class has dwindled down to nothing, but we don't have the heart to shut it down. He just loves to teach."

Right now, if you're serving in a ministry that's going nowhere, you need to be asking yourself some tough questions. Is it just a bad idea? Is it structurally flawed? Or are you just not the right person for the job? No one ever wants to admit that he's not the right person for the job, but sometimes it's the truth. Excellence requires that we serve in areas where we can do the most good . . . and the least harm.

Money

Third, excellence in ministry requires money. When I was first starting out in the ministry I made very little money, so I tried to cut corners and save wherever I could. One way I did this was by always buying inexpensive shoes. I tried never to pay more than twenty-five dollars. But then one day I started having trouble with my feet. They hurt when I walked, when I stood, and especially when I played sports. There were Sundays when I couldn't stand in the pulpit long enough to preach a sermon without my feet killing me.

In the back of my mind, I wondered if my shoes were the problem. Admittedly, they were flimsy and offered little support. So one day I walked into a shoe store and priced a top-of-the-line pair of dress shoes—and almost had a coronary. A nice pair of Florsheims cost almost one hundred dollars! I could buy three or four pairs of my old shoes for that amount of money. Not to mention the fact that I had barely one hundred dollars to my name.

I ended up buying those shoes, though spending so much money was a traumatic experience. I distinctly remember breaking out in a cold sweat as I handed the salesperson my money. But my purchase produced immediate results. When I wore those shoes, my feet didn't hurt at all. Today I may cut corners to save a buck here or there, but never on shoes. If you ever see me, look at my feet, and you'll see a pair of the finest shoes money can buy!

The simple truth is that quality costs. It's true with shoes and it's true in ministry, which is why some churches never achieve excellence in anything they do. They're too busy trying to save a dollar.

One church I know about decided to build a new building, and to build it as cheaply as possible. They had some good ol' boys in the congregation who owned some power tools, so they decided to do the bulk of the work themselves. They figured they could save tens of thousands of dollars.

But when the building was finished, you couldn't find a square corner in the place. Floors weren't level, doors didn't fit their frames properly, and light switches throughout the building were in the most inconvenient places. But the biggest problem was the plumbing. The toilets didn't flush properly and sewage constantly backed up in a downstairs drain, filling the entire building with a foul odor. The pastor and elders agreed the church would have been much better off to go ahead and spend the extra money up front and have the job done right.

If you're a key ministry person in your church—and especially if you have influence over how funds are spent—here are four facts you need to face:

Fact #1: Quality costs more, but generally pays for itself in the long run.
Fact #2: Quality equipment and resources will be a blessing to your servants.
Fact #3: High quality always makes a great first impression.
Fact #4: A commitment to quality says something about your love for the Lord.

Southeast Christian Church in Louisville, Kentucky, is a dynamic church that pushes twenty thousand in weekly worship attendance. They have a slogan we all should adopt: "If it bears His name, it's worth our best."[1] Remember that the next time the tightwads on your church board start insisting that the cheapest route be followed. There may be times when they'll be right. But if they are always allowed to have their way, the church will never achieve excellence.

Thorough Planning and Preparation

Fourth, excellence requires thorough planning and preparation. Baseball teams spend six weeks in spring training before they play their first game. Broadway shows spend months rehearsing before they ever do a live performance. Olympic athletes spend years in training before they ever compete for the gold medal. And doctors spend years in study and training before they are allowed to write their first prescription. What makes us think we can excel in the Lord's work without thorough planning and preparation?

One time a missionary speaker came to our church. I gave him a nice introduction and then he stepped to the podium and spoke words that made my blood boil. After greeting the people, he said, "I haven't had a lot of time to think about what I want to say tonight so I'm just going to let the Lord lead me." I wanted to stand up and say, "What do you mean you haven't had time to think about what you want to say? This speaking engagement was booked five months ago!" And yes, in case you're wondering, he did a terrible job. He rambled and stammered like someone who hadn't put any thought into his presentation. People all over the auditorium were nodding off. I might have, too, if my blood pressure hadn't been sky-high!

Sadly, that kind of thing happens way too often. I hate to say it, but some of the worst examples of public speaking I've ever heard have been in the church. Some of the sourest musical notes I've ever heard have been in the church. And some of the most embarrassing examples of mismanagement and disorganization I've ever observed have been in the church. And it isn't always because of a lack of ability. Far too often it's because people haven't adequately planned and prepared.

Several years ago, a pianist in the church I was serving (who was notorious for her lack of preparation) lectured me on this subject. She said, "Mark, you have everything so prepared ahead of time that it leaves no room for the Lord to move and inspire us. We can't possibly have any spontaneity in our services." I told her then (and I still believe) that concerns about spontaneity, while sometimes legitimate, are just as often an excuse for not planning and preparing. Have we forgotten that God has promised to honor and bless careful preparation? Proverbs 3:21–22 says, "My child, don't lose sight of good planning and insight. Hang on to them, for they fill you with life and bring you honor and respect" (NLT). And in all our concerns about inspiration and spontaneity, have we forgotten that God can do plenty of inspiring during the planning and preparation stage of an endeavor? Where is it written that God's Spirit moves and inspires only when the spotlights are turned on? And finally, whoever said that having a well-thought-out plan means you can't deviate if the Lord does move in a mighty way?

The bottom line is that a lack of preparation and planning in the Lord's work is the straightest road to mediocrity. *Nobody* is good enough to wing it all the time and keep producing topflight results. You show me a person who insists on flying by the seat of his pants in his service to the Lord, and I'll show you a solid candidate for membership in the Slipshod Hall of Fame.

Perseverance

And finally, excellence requires perseverance. Every day, people set out in the pursuit of noble goals, only to get discouraged and give up before they reach them. Maybe you recently blew your diet all to pieces by diving into a big pile of cheese fries. Or maybe you once started taking piano lessons with visions of Carnegie Hall dancing in your head, but never made it past "Mary Had a Little Lamb." Or maybe you've piled up quite a few college credits, but haven't ever gotten your degree. If so, you should now understand the value of perseverance.

The pursuit of excellence in ministry will always require perseverance because you will be surrounded by people who don't see things the way you do. You'll encounter people who have chosen mediocrity as a lifestyle. They're comfortable in it and will resent your efforts to change things. Keep in mind, some people have never risen above the level of mediocrity in *any* area of their lives. Forget church. They've settled for mediocrity at home, at work, and everywhere in between. So your passion for excellence is going to be very difficult for them to understand. They'll no doubt see you as some sort of weirdo fanatic.

Also, consider that some people who may have the best of intentions are simply blind to mediocrity, just as some people are blind to dirt. Have you noticed this? Some people are perfectly content to live in a dirty house. To them, it's comfortable. They're used to it. They literally do not see the filth. But when you walk in, you get the heebie-jeebies because you're accustomed to living in a clean environment. Likewise, the world is full of people who can look right at a slipshod, disorganized mess and not see a problem. If you start talking about changing it, they'll give you a blank stare and say, "Why?"

When you run into resistance, I encourage you to think about Jesus and the way He patiently taught and trained His disciples. It was a process that took three full years and brought many moments of frustration. We may read the Gospels and wonder how those guys could have been so thickheaded and slow to catch on. If you or I had been in Jesus' shoes, we might have fired them all and hired twelve new prospects. But we must remember that Jesus was calling them to a way of thinking and behaving that was entirely new to them. Nothing in their upbringing or experience had prepared them for what He was trying to teach them. Jesus understood this and adjusted His expectations accordingly.

Paul also understood the importance of perseverance when working toward change. While mentoring the young preacher Timothy, he said, "Preach the word of God. *Be persistent*, whether the time is favorable or not. *Patiently* correct, rebuke, and encourage your people with good teaching" (2 Timothy 4:2 NLT, emphasis added).

The question is not, *will* you meet resistance? The question is, what will be your response when you do? For the sake of the kingdom, I beg you not to give up. Hang in there and give your service to God your best effort. When others are slacking off, try harder. That extra effort you give might be the difference between some lost person being drawn in or driven away.

In Ecclesiastes 5:12, Solomon said, "People who work hard

sleep well" (NLT). When you first read that verse, you might think he's talking about fatigue—that when you work hard all day, you'll come home so exhausted you'll be able to fall into bed and be snoring in no time. But I don't think that's what he's saying at all. I believe he's talking about peace of mind. I believe he's saying that when you give any work your best effort, you'll have nothing to be ashamed of and no regrets. At that point, if you toss and turn in the night, it'll be because of that extra piece of pizza you ate, and not because of guilt.

People who work hard sleep well.

May we all have sweet dreams.

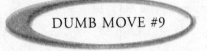

Allowing Wolves to Live Among the Sheep

Life for the wolves is death for the lambs.

—Isaiah Berlin

On September 15, 1999, the Wedgewood Baptist Church in Fort Worth, Texas, was hosting an area-wide youth rally. Jeff Laster was sitting in the church's south foyer talking to some other adults when a stranger walked into the building, smoking a cigarette. Jeff approached the man, both to greet him and to inform him that the church building was a nonsmoking facility. When he was about ten feet away, the stranger pulled out a 9mm pistol and shot him. From there, the gunman walked down a hallway and into the worship center, firing all the way. In the end, seven people were wounded and eight were killed, including the stranger, who took his own life.

I remember the day that story hit the news. I'm confident every

163

preacher in America reacted the way I did. I thought, *Is there no place sacred anymore? We've known for years that the streets, schools, restaurants, and office buildings of this country are not safe. Are we now going to have to add churches to that list?*

Shortly after that incident, I was preaching to my people on a Sunday morning. I was in the middle of my sermon when a man I had never seen before came walking down the center aisle. I kept talking, but my eyes were glued to the guy. The thought flashed through my mind that there was no logical reason for him to be approaching the pulpit at that moment, unless he intended to disrupt the service. I wondered if he was going to pull out a gun and shoot me. Several years earlier my family and I had been given police protection for a period of time because of some threats against my life. Even as I continued to preach, that ugly memory came rushing back with a vengeance. I later learned that a couple of our men who happened to be sitting on the aisle were watching the stranger closely and having similar thoughts. They told me that they were all set to tackle him if he even looked like he was about to pull out a gun.

Thankfully, the man reached the platform and knelt to pray in front of the pulpit. We later learned that he spoke no English and was deeply troubled. I'm sure he had no idea how much anxiety his little stroll down the aisle caused, or how close he had come to being flattened under about five hundred pounds of muscle!

Nowadays, churches are doing everything they can to prevent a repeat of what happened at Wedgewood Baptist. We understand that even a church lobby or a church sanctuary can become a killing field. In fact, with so much anti-Christian bias in our culture, we fully expect churches to become increasingly attractive targets for psycho killers. For this reason, many congregations have installed sophisticated alarm systems, trained security teams, and taught their members and staff to be sensitive to security issues. At Poinciana Christian Church, we even had a police presence one Sunday when some threats had been made against us.

Now let me tell you what *really* amazes me.

And what surely must frustrate God.

It's that we work so hard to protect our churches against physical enemies, but routinely allow spiritual enemies to come in and do their work unchallenged, week after week. I'm guessing that right now, in your very own church, there is at least one spiritual wolf, one troublemaker who has been responsible for a lot more pain and heartache than you realize. More likely, there are several. I'm talking about gossips, liars, caustic critics, legalists, and power-hungry manipulators—people who may never have performed an act of physical violence and, therefore, could never be arrested, but have still been responsible for untold suffering in the body of Christ.

And even some deaths.

Not physical deaths, of course, but spiritual ones. I can close my eyes and see the faces of numerous people I've known over the years who grew discouraged and eventually abandoned the faith because of a deep hurt they suffered at the hands of someone they ran into at church.

What's astonishing is that in many churches you'll find these people teaching classes, serving on boards and committees, greeting visitors at the front door, or even leading worship. Sometimes you'll even find these people on the paid staff!

WE'VE BEEN WARNED

When troublemakers rear their ugly heads in the church, there are always those who act surprised. I can't imagine why. Read the following statements from Jesus and the apostle Paul carefully:

> Beware of false prophets who come disguised as harmless sheep, but are really wolves that will tear you apart. You can detect them by the way they act, just as you can identify a tree by its fruit. (Jesus in Matthew 7:15–16 NLT)

> I know full well that false teachers, like vicious wolves, will come in among you after I leave, not sparing the flock. Even some of you will distort the truth in order to draw a following. Watch out! (Paul in Acts 20:29–31 NLT)

> These people are false apostles. They have fooled you by disguising themselves as apostles of Christ. But I am not surprised! Even Satan can disguise himself as an angel of light. So it is no wonder his servants can also do it by pretending to be godly ministers. (Paul in 2 Corinthians 11:13–15 NLT)

Jesus clearly warned us that wolves would invade the church, so, like Paul, we shouldn't be surprised. What we *should* be is prepared to meet the challenges they will bring. As any good military strategist will tell you, part of that preparation must come from knowing and understanding the enemy. Let me point out several facts about spiritual wolves that can be gleaned from the passages you just read.

FACT #1: SPIRITUAL WOLVES ARE MASTERS OF DECEPTION.

Obviously, if they walked in carrying a sign that said, "Watch out for me . . . I'm a troublemaker!" we'd fly into action. But they don't. Instead, they come in very quietly and respectfully, often giving the appearance of a humble, gentle seeker. Jesus said, "They come disguised as harmless sheep."

On this subject, let me offer an observation.

Don't be surprised if the biggest wolf in your church turns out to be the person you've helped the most. That's been the case in my experience more times than I could count. I'm not sure why this happens so often, except that we have a tendency to blindly embrace hurting and needy people. Maybe sometimes we embrace them a little too blindly. Remember that it's in a person's best interest to be very nice when he's in need and looking for help. He will almost always seem humble and grateful and willing to do whatever you ask. For that reason, you will likely find yourself being drawn to him. You will find yourself wanting to be the friend he's never had . . . the person who finally gives him a break. But watch out! When the crisis passes, he may well slip back into the same unhealthy behavior pattern that landed him in trouble in the first place. Never forget that it takes time to get to know people. What you see isn't always what you get. By rushing people into positions of influence before they have proved themselves, we can give wolves a foothold in the church.

FACT #2: SPIRITUAL WOLVES ARE DANGEROUS.

Jesus said they "will tear you apart" and Paul called them "vicious." It's sometimes very hard to believe this because wolves don't always look mean and nasty. I once knew a spiritual wolf who was more than seventy years old and didn't weigh a hundred pounds. She looked like somebody's sweet little grandma. But she was hands down the number one troublemaker in our church. Probably the worst gossip I have ever known.

FACT #3: SPIRITUAL WOLVES ARE EVIL. In 2 Corinthians 11, Paul minced no words. He came right out and said that the kind of troublemakers we're talking about are Satan's servants. This, I've noticed, is the one thing a lot of today's church leaders are reluctant to do. We don't mind saying that a person is "difficult" or "high-maintenance," but we'd rather not say he's evil. That would be unkind. And after all, the Bible tells us not to judge.

The problem is that when we fail to call evil by its name, we play right into the devil's hands. When we come up with softer, more politically correct terms to describe it, we minimize its seriousness and virtually guarantee that the behavior will continue. The early church leaders didn't hesitate to call evil by its name, and we shouldn't either.

FACT #4: SPIRITUAL WOLVES ALWAYS REVEAL THEMSELVES. Jesus said, "You can detect them by the way they act." Yes, they are masters of deception, but sooner or later they're going to show their true colors.

Keep one thing in mind, however.

We've all done wolfish things at one time or another. Therefore, it's never wise to label someone a wolf because of one incident. Perhaps the person was having an unusually bad day and was under a lot of stress. Or maybe he reacted without having all the information. If so, it's likely that his behavior, while troublesome, was not a reflection of his true character. We never want to become so rigid that we don't allow people to makes mistakes.

FACT #5: GOOD PEOPLE CAN MORPH INTO WOLVES. Isn't it amazing what moviemakers can do these days? With computer technology, they can morph a man into a monster right before your very eyes. Well, apparently, something like that occasionally happens in the church. In Acts 20, Paul was speaking to the elders, the godliest men in the Ephesian church. He warned them that wolves would be coming and then he added, "Even some of you will distort the truth in order to draw a following" (v. 30 NLT). That had to mean some of them were going to have to become wolves because there's no indication that they were wolves at that point.

Several years ago I served a church where one of the elders was a wolf. One day I was speaking to one of the former ministers of the church, and he expressed shock at the elder's behavior. He said, "When I worked there, he never behaved that way." There was no way to know why the man changed, but no one could deny that he had.

FACT #6: SPIRITUAL WOLVES LOVE POWER. Notice in the passages above that the wolves in question were said to be false prophets, teachers, and apostles. Nobody starts out from day one being a prophet, a teacher, or an apostle. Those are positions you work into over time, which tells us that wolves tend to be upwardly mobile. They're rarely content to come into a church and sit quietly while others make decisions. This, of course, is why they must be dealt with as soon as they are identified. The more influence they gain, the more damage they will do.

Maybe you've never considered the fact that spiritual wolves could actually be prowling the hallways of your church every Sunday and causing a lot of pain behind the scenes. You might be one of those people who just love to worship and serve quietly and aren't privy to a lot of inside information. If so, keep this in mind: Satan hates the church and will stop at nothing to hinder its work. Slipping a few wolves into the sheep pen would be the perfect way to accomplish that. We've been warned.

WE'VE BEEN HESITANT

Imagine for a moment that you're sitting in church on a Sunday morning. At the beginning of the service, the worship leader invites everybody to stand and sing. As you get to your feet, you see something you can hardly believe. The person directly in front of you has a pistol tucked into the waistband of his pants. As he leans forward to stand up, his shirttail rides up a little and you catch a glimpse of it.

What would you do?

I posed that question to several churchgoers from different congregations. Not one person said he or she would ignore the situation and go on singing. They all agreed they would slip out of their seats and go report the man with the gun.

Then I asked several church leaders what they would do if they received that report. They all agreed they would immediately call the authorities and see that the armed man was removed.

The question is, why don't we act with the same sense of urgency when we encounter spiritual threats to the safety of the flock? Why would we act quickly to remove a person who hasn't hurt anyone simply because he has a gun, but then hesitate to remove a man who's hurt a lot of people simply because he doesn't have a gun?

There are at least four reasons I have observed:

We Foolishly Believe People Will Change Without Discipline

Not long ago I was in a department store and found myself in the same aisle with a mom and her three- or four-year-old son. The boy picked up a trinket and asked his mother to buy it. When she said no, he immediately threw a screaming fit and only got louder when she tried to quiet him. Exasperated and embarrassed, she grabbed the toy and said, "Oh, okay. You can have it," which instantly put a smile on his face. Then she glanced at me, shrugged, and said, "I'll be glad when he outgrows this stage." I was tempted to say, "Lady, if you keep caving in and giving him whatever he wants every time he throws a fit, he's *never* going to outgrow it!"

Why do we think bad behavior will correct itself? History can produce no evidence that this ever happens. The Bible says that the more people sin and get away with it, the more they are inclined to keep on sinning (see Ecclesiastes 8:11).

Church leaders need to understand that a wolf preying on sheep is not going through a "stage." He's not going to wake up some morning and suddenly decide that he doesn't like the taste of lamb chops. He is a wolf, and he will do what wolves do until he is disciplined.

The Intertwining of Personal Relationships

A second reason why we hesitate to confront spiritual wolves is because of the intertwining of personal relationships. Recently, a pastor friend of mine called to talk (actually, to vent) about a horrific situation in his church. A young woman in the rural congregation he served had left her husband and children and hooked up with an unbeliever in a blatantly adulterous relationship. Her innocent husband and children were devastated, as you would expect. And not only was the church family in an uproar, the entire community was buzzing with gossip. The pastor's frustration, however, was directed at his elders. They had failed to take any disciplinary action and were intent on "waiting to see what happens."

Why?

Because the young woman was the senior elder's daughter.

He admitted that her actions were wrong, but insisted that, given enough time, she would come to her senses and return to her family. (As of this writing, she hasn't.) Sadly, the other elders, who were younger and less experienced, couldn't muster the courage to overrule the older leader. He had been a mentor to many of them, and they didn't want to "embarrass him further" by taking action against his daughter.

Isn't it true that we will allow our family members and close loved ones to get away with things we would never tolerate in strangers? We will make excuses for them and try to explain away their bad behavior. We'll plead for understanding and patience. And while we're doing that, they just keep right on soiling the family name.

We're Afraid of Collateral Damage

The third reason why we're often slow to deal with spiritual wolves is because we're afraid of the collateral damage. Troublemakers generally have family and friends in the church, and possibly in large numbers if they've been around for a while. So the very first thing the troublemaker will do when he's confronted is try to elicit sympathy and support from that group. As a way of making the church leaders regret taking action, he will try to draw as many people into the fracas as possible. He will go on a campaign to portray himself as a martyr. And if he ends up leaving the church, you can be sure he'll try to take a few people with him.

If he does, so be it.

Collateral damage is a fact of life.

You can't defeat an enemy in war without blowing up some perfectly good buildings. You can't destroy cancer cells in the human body without destroying a few healthy cells in the process. You can't restructure a business without having some employees get angry and quit. You can't take a church from stale traditionalism to vibrant growth without angering and losing a few members.

Church leaders must not be paralyzed by the fear of collateral damage. It is always true that greater damage is done in the long run if action isn't taken. The war will be lost. The cancer-infected body will die. The business will collapse. The stale church will continue to wither. And yes, the wolf will continue to feed on the sheep.

We Don't Know What to Do

But perhaps the biggest reason why we hesitate to take action against spiritual wolves is because we don't know what to do. This is not surprising. When was the last time you heard a sermon on the subject of church discipline?

Not long ago, Poinciana Christian Church withdrew fellowship from a spiritual wolf who was causing big trouble in the church and simply would not repent. Not long after that, someone expressed shock and said to me, "I've never heard of such a thing." Then it was my turn to be shocked because that person grew up in a preacher's home and had been attending church for more than seventy years!

In all honesty, I must admit that I am part of the problem. I, too, have rarely preached or taught on this subject. I, like most pastors, don't give it much thought until a wolf suddenly makes his presence known. Then I find myself wishing I'd talked about it more. I find myself wondering if a little more attention given to the subject would have at least caused the wolf to have second thoughts before attacking.

The good news is, we don't have to grope and stumble in the dark on this subject.

WE'VE BEEN INSTRUCTED

Before I address the process we've been instructed to follow, I want to say something about the spirit we've been commanded to maintain as the process unfolds. It should be one of gentleness and humility. Paul said, "Dear brothers and sisters, if another Christian is overcome by some sin, you who are godly should gently and humbly help that person back onto the right path. And be careful not to fall into the same temptation yourself" (Galatians 6:1 NLT).

This is a critical instruction because we generally get very angry when we see someone causing trouble in the church we love and have worked so hard to try to build. It's very easy for us to let our emotions get out of control. Then, first thing you know, we're escalating the rhetoric to nuclear levels and making harsh statements about the troublemaker that can never be taken back and that would probably make the person's repentance and restoration even less likely.

As Paul points out, this is also a time to be extra cautious about our own behavior. Satan would love nothing more than to see church leaders acting like the very wolves they're trying to deal with. And it can happen! When we get really ticked off, we can flash some serious claws and fangs of our own. The way to keep from crossing the line is to never lose sight of the primary goal. It's not to destroy the troublemaker, but to lead him back into a right relationship with God. Paul didn't instruct us to reject, repudiate, or resist the sinner, but to *restore* him. Most people think of church discipline as a negative thing (maybe that's why we rarely preach on the subject), but we must never forget its whole purpose is to bring about a positive result.

So what's the process?

Several passages offer valuable information, and they all need to be studied carefully. (They are Matthew 18:15–20; Romans 16:17; 1 Corinthians 5:1–13; 2 Corinthians 2:5–11; 2 Thessalonians 3:6–15; and 1 Timothy 1:18–20.) But there is one brief passage that serves as a sort of summary of the process God intends for us to follow when dealing with troublemakers. It's Titus 3:10–11, and it says, "If anyone is causing divisions among you, give a first and second warning. After that, have nothing more to do with that person. For people like that have turned away from the truth. They are sinning, and they condemn themselves" (NLT).

Let's draw six basic, but essential, conclusions:

CONCLUSION #1: NO ONE SHOULD GET A FREE PASS WHEN IT COMES TO BAD BEHAVIOR. Paul said that *anyone*

who is causing divisions in the church should be confronted. As I said before, sometimes we go easy on certain people because of who they are or who they're related to.

CONCLUSION #2: NOT ALL BAD BEHAVIOR MAKES A PERSON DESERVING OF CONFRONTATION OR REMOVAL FROM THE CHURCH.

Paul said that anyone who is causing divisions in the church should be confronted and removed if he doesn't repent. If you consider the other passages I listed above, you'll find that three other sins are specifically mentioned that could ultimately cause a person to be removed from the body. They were sexual immorality (see 1 Corinthians 5:1–5), a refusal to obey the apostles' teaching (see 2 Thessalonians 3:14), and a refusal to work (see 2 Thessalonians 3:6–10).

The point is, you don't confront somebody in this way just because he gets on your nerves. You don't confront somebody just because he disagrees with you. You don't confront somebody just because he's difficult or high-maintenance. If we were to do that, we'd never get anything else done because we're *all* difficult and high-maintenance at times!

CONCLUSION #3: BIBLICAL CHURCH DISCIPLINE IS A PROCESS, NOT AN ACT.

There must be a first and second warning with enough time built in for the offending person to show he either has or hasn't repented. Sometimes it takes awhile to know for sure. For example, I know of a case where a person was confronted about sexual sin. He seemed repentant and promised to change, but all he really did was start hiding it better. It wasn't until almost a year later that he slipped up and everyone learned he hadn't changed at all. That's when the second warning was given.

CONCLUSION #4: BIBLICAL CHURCH DISCIPLINE SHOULD BE CARRIED OUT WITH PATIENCE, BUT NOT TO AN EXTREME.

Paul says there should be a first and second warning, not a third, fourth, fifth, and sixth warning. In my experience, people who are going to repent will do so after the first warning. The second warning is critical because it shows patience and grace on the part of the leaders, but the first warning is generally the one that determines the outcome. Adding a third, fourth, or fifth warning simply prolongs the agony and undermines the authority of the church leaders by hinting that they don't have the courage to make a tough decision.

CONCLUSION #5: THE REMOVAL OF A PERSON FROM THE CHURCH'S FELLOWSHIP SHOULD BE THE LAST RESORT. I

love what Knofel Staton points out about the apostle Paul. He says, "Paul did not immediately think about disfellowshipping people because they did not agree with him. He did not even think about removal immediately when people were sinning. Instead, he wrote letters, prayed, made personal visits, and sent his helpers to be with the erring people. Discipline by removal was the last thing he wanted to do."[1]

When church leaders get to the place where they only want to see enemies removed, they will have become more like Hitler than Jesus. At all costs, we must keep love at the center of the process.

CONCLUSION #6: THERE SHOULD BE NO GUILTY FEELINGS ON THE PART OF CHURCH LEADERS WHO EXERCISE

CHURCH DISCIPLINE . . . AND NO ANIMOSITY DIRECTED TOWARD THEM BY MEMBERS OF THE CONGREGATION. Yes, there should be great sadness because any situation that requires this kind of response is tragic. But leaders shouldn't feel guilty, and members shouldn't be angry at the leaders for doing their jobs. Paul reminds us that those who are being disciplined are sinning and have "condemned themselves."

At this point I want to make sure you understand that even when a person "condemns himself" and is removed from the body, the door is never slammed and locked so that he can't return. Six months, a year . . . or even five or ten years later, he should be welcomed back into the fellowship if he comes to his senses and genuinely repents.

Remember when you were a child and were sent to your room for misbehaving? (I seem to have a lot of those memories.) What were the last words your mom spoke to you as she backed out of your room and closed the door? If she was like my mom, she said, "You can come out when you know how to act."

The same principle is at work when the process of church discipline reaches the final, removal stage. You're cutting the person off from fellowship with the rest of the family, praying that he will realize he's lost something wonderful because of his bad behavior. That realization often triggers a change of heart. When a child sits alone in his room and hears the rest of the family laughing and having a good time, he can become highly motivated to get his act together. And when a lonely believer sees a full parking lot as he drives by the church building . . . when he runs into one of his old friends from church at the grocery store or the bank . . . when he sees some members of his Bible school class having dinner together at a local restaurant . . . or when he no longer has anything to do on the night when he used to play softball with his buddies from the church, that's when he just might be motivated to rethink his behavior.

Removal always sounds harsh. In fact, I strongly recommend that you never talk about someone being "kicked out of the church." That type of terminology only perpetuates the notion that this is a vicious act. It isn't. It's a loving act. The same kind of action a parent would take with a beloved child.

To conclude this chapter, I want to tell you a story that I hope will provide encouragement for you at that moment when you realize a bloodthirsty wolf has infiltrated your flock.

When it happened to us, I literally felt sick to my stomach. A young woman had made a series of inappropriate advances toward a member of our staff. I say "inappropriate" because the staff member was married with children. At that point, the first warning was given. Instead of repenting, the woman became angry at the staff member for reporting the incidents and launched an all-out smear campaign against him. Terrible lies were being told, so the elders met with the woman again and issued a second warning. This resulted in such vile and wicked threats being made against the staff member and the church that we were forced to contact the sheriff's department. For the safety of everyone involved, the woman was restricted from setting foot on our church property at any time. At that point, the elders sent her a registered letter stating that she would not be welcome to return until she had fully repented and met with the elders to discuss her intentions.

Then came the hard part: telling the congregation.

Because the events mentioned above unfolded over a period of two or three days, not everyone had heard the woman's slanderous lies about the staff member and even fewer knew about the terrible threats she had made. Simply put, most of our members were clueless. We could have tried to keep the whole affair under wraps, but at Poinciana Christian Church our leadership philosophy is to be open with the congregation regarding problems of this nature. So the next Sunday morning at the end of our worship services, one of our elders read a statement. The problem was simply stated (minus the gory details), and the people were assured that the biblical pattern of church discipline had been followed to the letter. They were also informed that the individual would not be a part of our fellowship until she had fully repented. At that point, the elder asked that the people bow their heads and a prayer was offered for the woman. He prayed specifically that her heart would soften and that she would someday repent and return to her church family.

As the elder did his work, my thoughts went something like this:

I can't believe this is happening today of all days. We probably have more first-time guests in attendance this morning than we've had all year! What must they be thinking? Some of them have probably never heard of this process and will think our elders must take a gestapolike approach to church relations! And then there's the woman's friends. She's probably told them all sorts of lies to make the leadership look bad. It wouldn't surprise me if a bunch of them follow her out the door. When this is all said and done, there's no telling how many people we will have lost.

I'm happy to admit that I couldn't have been more wrong. The response of the congregation was so positive it almost brought me to tears. Person after person approached me and the other elders and thanked us for having the courage to do what they knew had to be a very difficult thing. Let me tell you about two couples in particular.

The first was a man and a woman who had just moved into our area and were looking for a church home. They approached me after the service and said, "We just want you to know that when your elder read the statement to the congregation, we knew we'd found our home. We've been in churches that have been torn apart by strife. We've been deeply hurt and are carrying a lot of scars. At this point in our lives, we want to find a place where we can feel safe—where we can have some confidence that the leaders take their responsibility to protect the flock seriously."

The other couple happened to be vacationing at Disney and stopped in our church for worship. They were both blinking back tears as they told me about how their church back home was being completely destroyed by warring factions. When they finished, they hugged me tightly and held on for a long time. They said, "God bless you and your elders for having the courage to stand up and do the right thing. If our elders had done it a year ago, our church wouldn't be in the mess it's in today."

Here's the lesson I learned.

As distasteful as the process of biblical church discipline is when you're going through it, the church *always* benefits. Like me, you'll probably envision all sorts of negative results, but when all is said and done, people want to be protected from the wolves of this world. People want to know that somebody somewhere is looking out for their best interests. And they respect courage. Whether they've ever been in a church leadership position or not, they instinctively know that dealing with troublemakers in the body of Christ is stressful and heartbreaking. They will love and respect those whose courage and commitment make it possible for them to live and worship in peace.

So please, don't be afraid to do what needs to be done.

It will be hard, but it will be worth it.

Accepting
the Unacceptable

Tolerance is the virtue of those who believe in nothing.
—RYAN DOBSON

It was the call no preacher wants to get.

An active member of our church phoned to tell me that her husband, also an active member, was having an affair with a coworker. She'd known only for a couple of hours, so she was still processing the information. As she spoke, her voice held a constant tremor, and she stopped to weep several times. After promising the church's help and support, I prayed with her and then asked where her husband was at that moment. She told me he was driving to work so I asked for his cell phone number. After jotting it down, I told her good-bye and dialed it. When he realized it was me, his voice became abnormally cheerful.

"Hey, Mark, what's goin' on?"

"Have you got a minute to talk?"

"I'm about ten minutes from work. What's up?"

"I just spoke to your wife," I said. "She told me some really disappointing news."

Silence.

"You know what I'm talking about, don't you?" I asked.

"We've been having a few problems."

"She told me you're having an affair. Is that true?"

There was another hesitation. Finally, he said, "Yes. I can't believe she told you."

"She was having trouble processing the information. She needed to talk to someone."

"When she and I talked about it earlier this afternoon, we agreed we'd work it out ourselves. It's nobody else's business."

"Listen, we need to talk," I said. "When can we get together?"

He hesitated. "I'm not sure. I don't know what my schedule is."

It was a lie. He knew exactly what his schedule was.

"We *really* need to talk," I said again.

"I'm going to have to get back to you after I check my schedule."

It was obvious that he wasn't going to agree to a meeting, so I pressed on to another topic—one that I never dreamed I'd ever have to address with him.

"I'm sorry," I said, "but I'm going to have to ask you to step down from your ministry until we can work through this situation and get it corrected."

He'd been on one of our key ministry teams for several years. He honestly seemed stunned.

"Why?"

"Why? I'd think the reason would be obvious."

"Because I'm a sinner?" he asked, with more than a touch of sarcasm in his voice. "Aren't you a sinner, Mark? Isn't everyone in the church a sinner? Why are you singling me out? Why don't you make everybody else step down from their ministries, too? Why don't you step down yourself?"

I couldn't believe what I was hearing.

"You can't be serious," I said.

"I'm dead serious," he countered. "What gives you the right to judge me?"

"Look," I said, trying to remain calm, "I'm not going to argue with you about this. You'll be relieved of your duties until you repent and get your life and your marriage back together."

"So, you're kickin' me out of the church?"

I sighed. "Come on. You know better than that."

But he said he didn't know better than that at all.

Then, just before he hung up, he pulled the pin on one more verbal grenade and lobbed it right into my lap. He said, "I don't think I even *want* to go to a church that kicks people when they're down. I'm having a few problems is all, and you're treating me like I'm some kind of ax murderer. Let me tell you what . . . you can go ahead and get someone to replace me permanently because I won't be back."

And, though he hadn't done so hot with his marriage vows, that was a promise he kept.

I wanted to share that conversation to start this chapter for one reason: I can remember a time when it never would have happened—when I never would have been asked to accept such unacceptable behavior.

I remember a time when everybody—even adulterers—

acknowledged that adultery was a sin. A time when even an unbeliever caught in an extramarital affair would have been embarrassed and ashamed. A time when apologies and excuses (or both) might have come gushing forth, but never the kind of smug defiance demonstrated by my friend.

When I replay that conversation in my mind, the words I hear most vividly are, "What gives you the right to judge me?"

That's the question everybody seems to be asking these days.

We live in a time when all the lines have been erased, all the fences have been knocked down, and all the forbidden fruit has been polished and set in a basket on the kitchen table. As the old Cole Porter jingle says, "In olden days a glimpse of stocking was looked on as something shocking. Now, heaven knows, anything goes!"

And that's *not* an exaggeration.

In January 2004, a German court sentenced Armin Meiwes to eight and a half years in prison for cannibalism. He'd placed an ad on the Internet looking for a well-built man who wanted to be killed and eaten, and a man named Bernd Brandes responded. The two men spent an evening getting to know each other, then Brandes agreed to be killed. In his testimony, Meiwes admitted that he didn't eat Brandes all at once, but defrosted cuts from his freezer over a period of several months.

But what's even more shocking than the story itself is the fact that so many people around the world rallied to Meiwes's defense. Both Meiwes and Brandes were seen as consenting adults who were merely exercising their freedom. Sure, their actions were a little bizarre, but if that's what they wanted to do, who are we to judge? Theodore Dalrymple wrote in *City Journal*, "By what right has the state interfered in their slightly odd relationship? Of course, one might argue that by eating Brandes, Meiwes was infringing on his meal's rights, and acting against his best interests. But Brandes decided that it was in his best interest to be eaten, and in general, we believe that the individual, not the state, is the best judge of his own interests."[1]

Such a story makes adultery seem blasé, doesn't it?

And that's the point.

The circle of acceptance has grown so large in our world that behaviors once on the outside are now on the inside. And behaviors once on the edge now appear to be in the center. This explains how a Christian (like my friend mentioned above) can commit adultery and then feel offended when someone tries to hold him accountable.

But that's not all it explains.

It also explains why the church is having so little impact on culture. You'd think that in a society where almost four in ten adults claim to be born-again Christians, there would be an explosion of opposition against such things as:

- abortion,
- the redefining of marriage,
- the peddling of sex and violence to children,
- the granting of special rights to homosexuals,
- the constant promotion of humanism in our schools,
- the teaching of evolution to children as scientific fact,
- and the relentless belittling of any Christian who dares to express his or her faith in the public arena.

But, not Christians, for the most part, have been disengaged as these dangerous trends have picked up steam. As a friend of mine quipped, "We haven't just been quiet, we've been comatose!" God must be sighing and shaking His head at our complacency.

WE NEED TO WAKE UP

In Matthew 13:24–25, Jesus sets up a parable this way:

> The Kingdom of Heaven is like a farmer who planted good seed in his field. But that night as everyone slept, his enemy came and planted weeds among the wheat. (NLT)

Notice two things about the enemy.

First, he's calculating. He waits until the farmer and his farmhands are in bed sawing logs before he makes his move.

Second, he's conniving. He knows, for example, that if he tries to set the farmer's field on fire, the farmer will wake up and fly into action. So he chooses instead to walk through the farmer's field dropping weed seed. That way, even if the farmer gets up in the middle of the night for a glass of warm milk and spots him, he looks like just another harmless passerby traveling at night to avoid the heat of the day. Only later, when his enemy is long gone, will the farmer discover that he has a weed problem and realize he's been had.

This is a perfect picture of how Satan works. He understands that a diminished crop is the next best thing to a destroyed crop. And in one way it's better. A diminished crop has the added benefit of leaving the farmer to feel like a complete fool for not paying closer attention.

A mom named Mary knows the feeling.

Not long ago, it was widely reported that one of the nation's biggest-selling computer games, *Grand Theft Auto*, could be modified to include scenes of hard-core pornography. By installing software available over the Internet, a player would be allowed to engage in a variety of sex acts with a character known as "the girlfriend."

Mary never gave a thought to the games her fourteen-year-old son was playing until she saw that report. Suddenly, her curiosity was aroused and she started snooping. To her surprise, she found *Grand Theft Auto* in her son's collection. She was dumbfounded to learn that even without the infamous modification, the game still allowed players to kill police officers, run down pedestrians, and engage prostitutes. Alarmed, she questioned her son and learned that he'd been playing the game for two years. When she asked where he got it, he calmly informed her that *she* had given it to him for Christmas!

Do you see how Mary's experience mirrors that of the farmer in Jesus' parable? The enemy snuck in when she wasn't paying attention. Not to try to destroy her son in one grand act of violence, but just to sow some weed seed. She couldn't remember the exact day she purchased the game, but she assumed it was when she was on one of those Christmas-shopping blitzes that had her running here and there all day long, trying to mark as many things off her list as possible. That's undoubtedly why she hadn't taken the time to really look at the game. She'd heard her son talk about it. Some of his friends owned it. Surely, *their* parents had checked it out.

Unless, of course, they weren't paying attention either.

But that night as everyone slept, his enemy came . . .

Right now, before it's too late, somebody needs to sound the alarm.

Fire the cannons.

Blow the trumpets.

Bang on the pots and pans.

Pull the string on the foghorn.

Whatever it takes to snap Christians awake.

For too long, the enemy has been creeping virtually un-challenged through our culture sowing weed seed. He's been so successful for so long that the weeds are starting to look like they belong. People are starting to think weeds are pretty. They're start-ing to prefer weeds over wheat. Some are even pulling up the wheat to make room for more weeds.

If ever we needed to wake up, the time is now.

But that's not all.

WE NEED TO SPEAK UP

It was a sixteen-hour period that residents of Montgomery County, Maryland, will never forget.

- At 6:04 p.m., James D. Martin, 55, was shot and killed outside a grocery store.
- At 7:41 the next morning, James "Sonny" Buchanan, 39, was shot and killed as he mowed grass.
- At 8:12 a.m., Premkumar Walekar, 54, was shot and killed as he refueled his cab at a Mobil station.
- At 8:37 a.m., Sara Ramos, 34, was shot and killed as she sat on a bench in front of a post office.

◻ And at 9:58 a.m., Lori Ann Lewis-Rivera was shot and killed at a Shell station as she vacuumed the interior of her minivan.

You may remember that these and nine other people were randomly gunned down in the Washington, D.C, area during October 2002. Eventually, John Allen Muhammed and Lee Boyd Malvo were charged with the crimes and convicted. Their intent was apparently to try to extort millions of dollars through terrorism. You probably also remember that you couldn't turn on the television during that three-week reign of terror without hearing warnings being issued to people living in that area. Gas stations and strip malls were where most of the shootings seemed to be taking place, so people were urged to avoid such places if at all possible and stay indoors until the snipers could be apprehended.

If there's one thing we do very well in America, it's warn people about physical danger:

◻ When a case of mad cow disease crops up . . .
◻ When a hardened criminal escapes from prison . . .
◻ When a hurricane is bearing down on American soil . . .
◻ When questions arise about the safety of a well-known drug . . .
◻ Or when someone goes on a shooting rampage, we hear all about it.

But those same news outlets that do such a great job of warning us about physical danger rarely warn us about spiritual danger. One example of a time when they did would be the porn-enhanced computer game *Grand Theft Auto*, which I mentioned earlier. But for the most part, the secular media is quiet when it comes to the dangers that threaten our souls. I believe there are two reasons for this. One, their secular worldview doesn't allow them to see through the eyes of faith. And two, they figure it's not their job; it's the church's.

I agree wholeheartedly. Read the following passage carefully.

> I have appointed you as a watchman for Israel. Whenever you receive a message from me, pass it on to the people immediately. If I warn the wicked, saying, "You are under the penalty of death," but you fail to deliver the warning, they will die in their sins. And I will hold you responsible, demanding your blood for theirs. If you warn them and they keep on sinning and refuse to repent, they will die in their sins. But you will have saved your life because you did what you were told to do. (Ezekiel 3:17–19 NLT)

This was God's commission to the prophet Ezekiel, but it should be taken to heart by every Christian. When Jesus told us to let our lights shine, He was instructing us to expose the things of darkness. When He told us to spread the good news, He knew we wouldn't be able to do it without confronting the bad news. God has always intended for His people to be watchmen and to speak up when danger appears. Hebrews 3:13 says, "You must warn each other every day, as long as it is called 'today,' so that none of you will be deceived by sin and hardened against God" (NLT).

But often we don't warn one another.

Isaiah 56:10 is a stinging indictment of Israel's leaders, and it could be justifiably leveled at many modern Christians. It says,

"For the leaders of my people—the LORD's watchmen, his shepherds—are blind to every danger. They are like silent watchdogs that give no warning when danger comes" (NLT).

What a perfect description of far too many of us. We're like watchdogs lying on the rug, watching burglars carry off half the house. We raise our heads, offer a halfhearted "Woof!" then figure we've done our jobs. What we need to do is spring to our feet, bare our teeth, and bark our heads off at the first hint of danger. History shows that if enough of us will do that, the thieves will turn tail and run.

In 2003, the clothing store chain Abercrombie & Fitch came out with a Christmas catalog that featured nude models in sexual poses. Some of the pictures even simulated group sex. The catalog also contained advice from a sex expert encouraging young people (which they cater to almost exclusively) to broaden their sexual experiences, even to the point of trying threesomes.

Thankfully, an attentive watchdog named Joe Gibbs saw the catalog and started barking. The NFL coach and NASCAR owner called James Dobson and told him what he'd discovered. Then Dobson started barking! He immediately went on his radio show and urged listeners to call Abercrombie & Fitch and tell them they were boycotting their products until the catalog was removed. Then his listeners started barking! The company started receiving three hundred phone calls per hour from all over the country.

Want to guess what happened?

On the day before Thanksgiving, Abercrombie & Fitch pulled the catalog from all 651 of its stores. Oh, sure, they said it had nothing to do with the boycott. They said they needed to make room on the counter for a new perfume display.[2]

Yeah, right.

They can say what they want, but you and I both know they pulled the catalog because of all the barking watchdogs.

And this is what makes our silence so tragic. Good things happen when God's people wake up and speak up. That's what James was getting at when he said, "Resist the Devil, and he will flee from you" (James 4:7 NLT). Notice, he doesn't say Satan might flee or could flee; he says Satan *will* flee. We have a promise from God that Satan is a coward . . . that he will hightail it out of there when God's people show some resistance to his evil schemes.

But let me offer a word of caution.

Yes, we need to wake up and speak up.

Yes, we need to bark like crazy when confronted with the unacceptable.

But, in the process, we must never forget to reflect the heart and character of Christ. Our calling is to "[speak] the truth in love" (Ephesians 4:15 NKJV). We accomplish nothing for the kingdom if we act mean and hateful. Our job is to bark, not maul.

When I was in high school, I worked for a furniture store. One day my boss and I were delivering a sofa to a farmhouse. As we carried the sofa across the lawn, the family's German shepherd came charging around the corner of the house, barking for all he was worth. I'm like most people in that barking dogs don't bother me, but biting dogs do. So I started getting worried when I saw that he was bearing down on me at full speed. I kept thinking/hoping he would pull up short, but no, he sank his teeth into my lower right leg like it was a chunk of raw meat. Before the owner could pull him off, my jeans were torn and I had bloody teeth marks on my leg.

How do you think I feel about German shepherds today?

I'll give you one guess.

You're right. I don't like them. It gives me the heebie-jeebies to be around them. And the world will feel the same way about us if we stop being watchdogs and become attack dogs. Quite frankly, they'll hate us. They'll see us as unstable, wild-eyed fanatics. And never, under any circumstances, will they take anything we have to say seriously.

Remember that Jesus managed to speak openly about sin and effect change in His culture, while still managing to have a friendly relationship with many hard-core sinners. He never compromised the truth. In fact, some of His comments were so pointed they still make us cringe to this day. Yet many sinners were drawn to Him. They even invited Him to their parties (see Luke 5:29)! There's only one way that could possibly have happened. He had to have had love dripping off Him at all times.

One thing that will help you in this regard is to remember that while watchdogging is critically important, especially in an age when Satan has so many subtle techniques at his disposal, it's not our primary mission. Our primary mission as servants of Christ is to seek and to save the lost (Luke 19:10 NIV). So anytime you find yourself in a situation where you feel you need to speak up, ask yourself how you can do it in the least offensive way possible. There just might be someone within earshot who is secretly curious about the Lord they see you serving so passionately. Don't blow that opportunity by being needlessly mean and hateful.

We need to wake up.

We need to speak up.

And one more thing . . .

WE NEED TO SHAPE UP

If we're going to impact our communities and our culture in a positive way, we simply must put some walk behind our talk. When we act outraged at the world's values and then are caught living on the same level, we come off looking like fools.

I'll never forget the time I went to visit a new family in our church. I'd noticed that they were quite vocal about their faith, so I wasn't surprised when I walked into their home and saw a family Bible on the coffee table and a decorative plaque on the wall that quoted Joshua's famous statement, "As for me and my house, we will serve the Lord."

But I did get a shock when I sat down.

I settled into a recliner that was positioned near a large bookcase. It just so happened that on the shelf that was exactly level with my eyes, there was a row of about thirty or forty videos. When I turned my head, they weren't more than three feet away, so I could read the titles easily. I did a double take when I saw a movie that was well-known as an R-rated cop caper. As my eyes moved on down the row, I realized that this was a genre the family obviously enjoyed. At least half the movies were R-rated, and, judging from the titillating titles, about half of them were what the movie industry would call "hard R's."

All that evening, that husband and wife talked to me about their faith and their convictions. But I have to say, none of it really resonated with me. In fact, as I listened my mind wandered. I kept imagining myself reaching over and pulling one of those movies off the shelf, holding it up, and saying, "If you've got such strong convictions, then how do you explain *this*?" But of course, I didn't do that. I just listened and smiled and nodded. And felt a little ill.

Now, I'm not saying that man and his wife are going to hell because they own some R-rated movies. Not at all. But I do believe the choice they've made to enjoy that type of entertainment muddies their witness. It reminds me of the story about a mom who took a batch of homemade applesauce and a batch of homemade cottage cheese to a church social. As long as she was doing the dipping, everything was fine. The trouble started when she left her little boy in charge. He used the same spoon for both, so it wasn't long before there was so much cottage cheese in the applesauce and so much applesauce in the cottage cheese that you couldn't tell which was which. And nobody wanted either one!

In 2 Timothy 2:21, Paul said, "If you keep yourself pure, you will be a utensil God can use for his purpose. Your life will be clean, and you will be ready for the Master to use you for every good work" (NLT).

If you keep yourself pure . . .

Five little words.

Only twenty-one letters.

But together they explain why the church has so little influence in our culture. Look at this statement from Erwin Lutzer:

Opinion polls show that the difference between the church and the world is, in some ways, indistinguishable. The sins that are in the world are in the church: divorce, immorality, pornography, risqué entertainment, materialism, and apathy toward what others believe. Officially, we believe that without trusting Jesus as Savior people are lost. Unofficially, we act as if what people believe and the way they behave really does not matter. No wonder our light has become a flicker and our salt has lost its savor.[3]

So many Christians today remind me of what the Bible says about Amaziah, one of Judah's kings. He was twenty-five years old when he rose to power, and he reigned for twenty-nine years. But his one-sentence epitaph is stained by a very sad observation. Second Chronicles 25:2 says, "Amaziah did what was pleasing in the LORD's sight, but not wholeheartedly" (NLT).

Halfhearted or three-quarter-hearted Christianity is what allows Satan to win so many of the confrontations that happen in our culture. For example, it never ceases to amaze me that so many Christians fail to vote. The right to vote is one of the most powerful weapons believers have. If God's people ever rose up as one and took advantage of this wonderful privilege, we could bring about huge changes in the direction of our culture. But every Election Day the story is the same. An alarming number of us stay home.

After the last national election, I happened to be talking to a man in our church who confessed to me that he didn't vote. The first thing that popped into my mind was the infamous Super Bowl halftime show when Janet Jackson's breast was exposed during a dance number. I remembered that the next morning the same man had gone off on a rant about the decline of morals in our culture. So he can rant, but he can't vote. Do you see the problem? Our inconsistencies are maddening. Halfheartedness is ruining any chance we might have of shrinking the circle of acceptance.

In Matthew 7:3–4, Jesus said, "Why worry about a speck in your friend's eye when you have a log in your own? How can you think of saying, 'Let me help you get rid of that speck in your eye,' when you can't see past the log in your own eye?" (NLT). Those verses couldn't be more relevant to the modern church. We need to save our complaining about the world until after we have cleaned up our own house.

I am fully aware that the circle of acceptance in our world is always going to be larger than we want it to be. However, I do believe it could be shrunk. History indicates that some very negative and harmful trends could be stopped and perhaps reversed if enough of us would wake up, speak up, and shape up.

Perhaps you've noticed that we live in a world of alliances. Corporations merge in an effort to blow away the competition. Nations align themselves with one another to fight a common enemy, such as terrorism. Political action groups team up to support or defeat a candidate. And artists and entertainers collaborate to create best-selling music and movies. But by far the most powerful alliance the world will ever know is that of the Lord and His people. Throughout history we have seen that when God and His children get on the same page and join forces, amazing things happen. There was even a time when the enemies of the faith acknowledged that our alliance had turned the world upside down (see Acts 17:6).

I think it's high time we did it again.

And we could, if we'd quit accepting the unacceptable.

A Letter from Mark

Dear Reader,

Thank you for taking the time to read this book. If you've read any of my others, you know this one is a little different. No, I haven't lost my passion for great Bible stories and characters, but I did feel the Lord leading me to temporarily step away from them and tackle a subject that few other voices are addressing.

Edward R. Murrow once said, "Most truths are so naked that we feel sorry for them and cover them up, at least a little." I feel that way about the truths in this book. Though I've tried to approach them with grace and humor, they are still quite naked and raw. So much so that a friend of mine was scanning the table of contents and said, "I feel convicted just reading the chapter titles!" Naked truth has a way of making you squirm. It can make you want to throw a sheet over it.

Ordinarily, I am not the whistle-blower type. I'm not the guy who grabs the sheet and jerks it away. Exposing nakedness is not my thing. But in this case, I had no choice. I knew that once the Lord put this message on my heart, there was no point in fighting it. I'm thankful my friends at Nelson Books agreed this was a topic that needed to be addressed.

I must tell you that this has been one of the more difficult books I've written, probably because I've so often been a blundering believer myself. But now that it's finished, I feel more than just the glow of satisfaction that comes from finishing a yearlong writing project. I somehow feel changed . . . like something happened to me along the way. Time will tell, but I feel that from now on, I stand the chance of being at least a little less clumsy in my Christian walk. My greatest wish for this book is that it would bring out similar feelings in you. A few less dumb moves from all of us would no doubt create more joy in heaven, less snickering in hell, and a church that more closely resembles what God always intended it to be.

I'd love to hear any feedback you'd like to offer. My e-mail address is MarkAtteberry@aol.com.

In His Love,

Mark

Questions for Group Discussion or Personal Reflection

Dumb Move #1: Slinging Mud on the Bride of Christ

1. Of the four kinds of mudslingers mentioned—the missing, the malcontents, the moochers, and the misbehavers—which group do you feel has slung the most mud in your church? Is it possible that some people in your church see you as belonging to one of these groups?

2. Think of the last time you heard someone make a disparaging comment about your church. What was said? How did you respond? If you had it to do over again, would you respond differently? How?

3. If you were unhappy about something or someone in your church, would you be more likely to keep quiet or speak up? If you chose to speak up, who would you talk to and why? Have you done this in the past? What was the result?

Dumb Move #2: Winning People to the Church Rather Than to the LORD

1. When you witness, do you have a tendency to talk more about your church than the Lord? When you come into contact with a stranger, are you more likely to ask him if he goes to church or if he is saved? Why?

2. How has your church changed since you first became a member? When you first joined, did anybody warn you to expect changes? How well have you coped with the changes that have occurred?

3. Do you know any people who left your church because of changes that have occurred? Do you feel they were justified in doing so?

4. What personal experience could you share with people that would illustrate how Jesus is your Way? Your Truth? Your Life?

Dumb Move #3: Living Below the Level of Our Beliefs

1. Of the three sins mentioned in this chapter—materialism, worry, and an attitude of superiority—which one have you found is the most likely to fly under your radar and take up residence in your life? Could you add others to the list? What would they be?

2. How do you feel about current preaching trends? Have you ever been jolted to your senses by a single sermon? Who was the preacher? What was the topic? How did you change your behavior as a result?

3. Proverbs 4:23 says, "Above all else, guard your heart, for it affects everything you do" (NLT). What are some practical things you can do to keep your heart from growing insensitive to sin?

Dumb Move #4: Speaking Above the Level of Our Knowledge

1. Have you ever expressed a negative opinion of someone, only to discover sometime later that you were completely mistaken? Have you ever passed on a juicy bit of information, only to discover later that it was not true?

2. Have you ever been the victim of a mischaracterization? What was said about you? How did it affect you? What did you do about it? How was your relationship with the person who made the comment affected?

3. Historically, Christians have been quick to spread misinformation (such as the lie about J. K. Rowling being a witch). Why do you think that is? What precautions can we take to keep ourselves from making this mistake?

Dumb Move #5: Hopping from Church to Church

1. Have you ever switched churches without changing your residence? Why did you do it? How difficult was it? Did you find what you were looking for? If you had it to do over, would you make the same decision?

2. Have you ever resisted the temptation to switch churches? What made you think about changing? Why didn't you make the change? Are you glad you stayed put?

3. What do you feel would be some legitimate reasons for leaving one church and joining another?

4. What would be some illegitimate reasons?

Dumb Move #6: Fighting Among Ourselves

1. Have you ever been deeply hurt by another Christian? How did that injury affect your walk with the Lord? Have you forgiven the person who hurt you? What is your relationship with that person today?

2. Church conflicts are minimized when the members of the church are submissive to the leadership. Can you think of a time when you disagreed with the leadership, but chose to be

submissive for the sake of peace? How difficult was it for you to do that? How do you feel about that choice today?

3. Jesus said to the church in Ephesus, "But I have this complaint against you. You don't love me or each other as you did at first!" (Revelation 2:4 NLT). What about your church? Is it as warm and loving as it used to be? Have you noticed an increase in conflict? If so, why do you think this is happening? What, specifically, can you and some of your friends do to tip the balance back the other way?

Dumb Move #7: Missing Golden Opportunities

1. Have you ever let a golden opportunity slip through your fingers? Why didn't you seize it? Were you not paying attention? Were you afraid? Were you lazy? What do you feel you could have missed as a result?

2. Some opportunities are larger than they first appear. Can you think of a time when you seized what you thought was a small opportunity, only to have it produce a huge result?

3. One of the reasons we miss opportunities to serve is because people are such good actors. What about you? Do you pretend to be happy and healthy even when you're hurting?

4. How could you be more genuine about your needs without becoming a chronic complainer?

Dumb Move #8: Settling for Mediocrity

1. When the subject of excellence comes up, what's the first thing you think of?

2. Name some areas where you feel your church demonstrates excellence. Are there some areas where you feel improvement is

needed? What, specifically, could you do to improve the quality of those areas?

3. Have you ever made a decision to pursue excellence and suffered criticism as a result? What was the specific complaint that was leveled against you? Did you back off or stick to your guns?

4. To serve with excellence, you must serve in the area of your giftedness. Think about your current ministry involvement. Do you feel your gifts are being maximized? If not, why? What could you do to change that?

Dumb Move #9: Allowing Wolves to Live Among the Sheep

1. Can you remember a time when the leaders of your church practiced biblical church discipline? What was the reaction of the people? In what ways do you feel the church benefited?

2. Can you remember a time when disciplinary action should have been taken and wasn't? In what ways do you feel the church was harmed?

3. The Bible tells us not to judge, but it also tells us to confront troublemakers in the church. How would you resolve what some people say is a conflict between these two commands? At what point does a person's behavior "cross the line" and become worthy of discipline?

4. The fear of collateral damage keeps some church leaders from taking action against troublemakers. Can you think of a situation where it might be better to leave the trouble maker alone rather than risk splitting the church down the middle? Explain.

Dumb Move #10: Accepting the Unacceptable

1. Do you find yourself being more tolerant of worldly fads and trends than you used to be? Can you name some that used to bother you a great deal, but that you rarely notice anymore?

2. If someone who didn't know you walked through your house and looked through your things, would he find contradictions, such as a family Bible on the coffee table right next to a shelf full of R-rated movies? If contradictions like this do exist in your life, are you willing to eliminate them?

3. God's promise is that Satan is a coward . . . that he will flee if we resist him. Can you name some specific ways you have resisted him in the past? Do you vote? Have you ever participated in a boycott? What else could you do to show that you will not accept the unacceptable?

Notes

Dumb Move #4: Speaking Above the Level of Our Knowledge

1. http://freaky_freya.tripod.com/misinformation.html, accessed January 27, 2005.
2. Mark Matlock, *Don't Buy the Lie* (Grand Rapids: Zondervan, 2004), 105.

Dumb Move #5: Hopping from Church to Church

1. Joshua Harris, *Stop Dating the Church* (Sisters, OR: Multnomah, 2004), 17.
2. Rick Warren, *The Purpose Driven Church* (Grand Rapids: Zondervan, 1995), 324.

Dumb Move #6: Fighting Among Ourselves

1. Steve Coll, *Washington Post*, December 5, 2004.

Dumb Move #7: Missing Golden Opportunities

1. Floyd McElveen, *Unashamed* (Sisters, OR: Multnomah, 2003), 118.
2. Ibid., 120–21.

Dumb Move #8: Settling for Mediocrity

1. Bob Russell, *When God Builds a Church* (West Monroe: Howard Publishing, 2000), 107.

Dumb Move #9: Allowing Wolves to Lie Among the Sheep

1. Knofel Staton, *God's Plan for Church Leadership* (Cincinnati: Standard Publishing, 1982), 113.

Dumb Move #10: Accepting the Unacceptable

1. Charles Colson, *Lies That Go Unchallenged* (Wheaton: Tyndale, 2005), 34.
2. Colson, *Lies That Go Unchallenged*, 235–37.
3. Erwin Lutzer, *Who Are You to Judge?* (Chicago: Moody, 2002), 15–16.

About the Author

Mark Atteberry loves living in central Florida with his wife, Marilyn. In addition to preaching and writing, his great passions are sports and music. Mark loves to hear from his readers and invites you to contact him by e-mail at MarkAtteberry@aol.com. Visit his website at markatteberry.net.